Human Roots

Buddhist Stories for Young Readers

Adapted &
Translated into English by
Dharma Realm Buddhist University,
Buddhist Text Translation Society
Talmage, California & 1983

Volume Two

HUMAN ROOTS: Buddhist Stories for Young Readers

VOLUME 2

All stories in this volume are true accounts of past events
involving Buddhas, Bodhisattvas, Arhats, sages, and other
great beings. They have been compiled from the Tripitaka,
public records, and historical accounts.

Translated by the BUDDHIST TEXT TRANSLATION SOCIETY,
DHARMA REALM BUDDHIST UNIVERSITY.

Adapted and compiled by:Bhikshunis Heng Wen and Heng Ming
"Story of Cause and Effect" adapted by Upasaka David Rounds

Edited by:Bhikshus Heng Sure Ph.D. and Heng Ch'au Ph.D.

Certified by: Venerable Abbot Hua and Bhikshuni Heng Tao Ph.D.

ISBN: 0-88139-017-8
Copyright© 1984 by DHARMA REALM BUDDHIST ASSOCIATION,
DHARMA REALM BUDDHIST UNIVERSITY.

ACKNOWLEDGEMENTS:

Typing: Bhikshunis Heng Ming, Heng Liang, Heng Bin, and
          Marlene Ma

Drawings by: Bhikshuni Heng Ming and BTTS staff
             Upasaka Abel Traullé

Layout: Bhikshuni Heng Ming

Proofing: Bhikshus Heng Shun and Heng Tso, Bhikshunis Heng
            Chu, Heng Liang, and Heng Chia, Upasikas Susan
            Rounds and Marion Robertson

FOR INFORMATION AND BOOK SALES CONTACT:

City of Ten Thousand Buddhas
P.O. Box 217
Talmage, Ca. 95481
Tel. (707)462-0939
(Book order Headquarters)

Gold Mountain Monastery
1731 15th Street
San Francisco, Ca. 94103
Tel. (415)626-4204
     (415)861-9672

Gold Wheel Monastery
1728 West 6th Street
Los Angeles, Ca. 90017
Tel. (213)483-7497

Buddhist Text Translation Society
Eight Regulations

A translator must free himself or herself from the motives of personal fame and reputation.

A translator must cultivate an attitude free from arrogance and conceit.

A translator must refrain from aggrandizing himself or herself and denigrating others.

A translator must not establish himself or herself as the standard of correctness and suppress the work of others with his or her faultfinding.

A translator must take the Buddha-mind as his or her own mind.

A translator must use the wisdom of the Selective Dharma Eye to determine true principles.

A translator must request the Elder Virtuous Ones of the ten directions to certify his or her translations.

A translator must endeavor to propagate the teachings by printing sutras, shastra texts, and vinaya texts when the translations are certified as being correct.

南無本師釋迦牟尼佛

Namo Shakyamuni Buddha

TABLE OF CONTENTS

Human Roots

~Volume Two~

KUMARAJIVA

Kumarajiva is the name of the Indian monk who translated the AMITABHA SUTRA from Sanskrit into Chinese. Even when he was young, he had the wisdom and virtue of a much older person.

When Kumarajiva was seven years old, his mother took him to a temple to worship the Buddha. Kumarijiva picked up a large bronze incense urn and easily lifted it up over his head. Then he thought, "Hey! I'm just a child. How can I lift this heavy urn?" As soon as he had this false thought, the urn crashed to the ground. This experience taught him the meaning of the saying, "Everything is made from the mind alone." It was not long before he and his mother both left the home life.

1

Even though Kumarajiva's father was a cultivator himself, he didn't want his wife--Kumarajiva's mother--to leave home. In order to get him to agree to let her leave home, Kumarajiva's mother began to fast. "Unless you allow me to leave home," she said, "I won't eat or drink. I'll starve myself."

For six days she didn't eat or drink, not even fruit juice, and she became extremely weak. Finally her husband said, "This is too dangerous. You are going to starve to death. You may leave home, but first please eat something."

"First call in a Dharma Master to cut off my hair," she said. "Then I'll eat." So a Dharma Master came and shaved her head, and then she ate.

3

Shortly after leaving home, she certified to the third fruit of Arhatship

Soon after that, Kumarajiva also left home. Everyday he read and recited many Sutras, and once he read them, he never forgot them. Because he had such a fine memory, he was very good at debating. He won debates with all the non-Buddhist philosophers, and he became very famous.

His reputation even spread to China. The Emperor wanted to bring Kumarajiva to China. So he sent a great general with 70,000 soldiers to India to capture Kumarajiva and take him to China. Kumarajiva knew what was happening. He told the King of his own country: "The Emperor of China is sending a big army here. But don't fight them. They don't want to take over your country. They have another reason for coming here." He knew that they just wanted to bring him back to China with them.

But unfortunately, the King didn't listen to Kumarajiva, and he sent his army to fight the army from China. As a result, the King was killed, his army was defeated, and Kumarajiva was captured.

On the way back to China, the Chinese general was preparing to camp in a low valley. Kumarajiva, who had spiritual powers, knew that a rain was coming which would flood the valley. He told the general, "Don't camp here tonight. This place is dangerous."

But the general did not believe him. "You're a monk," he said. "What do you know about the military affairs?"

That night there was a torrential rainstorm, and many men and horses were drowned. Then the general realized that Kumarajiva was no ordinary person.

When Kumarajiva got to China, he began to translate Sutras from Sanskrit into Chinese. More than eight hundred bhikshus came to help him with these translations. Kumarajiva translated scores of Sutras during his lifetime. His translations are extremely elegant and so people have read them throughout many generations.

AFTER YOU READ

1. Why did Kumarajiva go to China?
2. How did Kumarajiva's mother get her husband to agree to let her leave home?
3. Why did Kumarajiva drop the urn?
4. What made the Chinese general realize that there was something special about Kumarajiva?

6

Kumarajiva's mother certified to the third Fruit of Arhatship. What does that mean? What are the other fruits of Arhatship?

Kumarajiva was well known for his excellent memory. How good is your memory? Ask your teacher to help you choose something to memorize and see how quickly you can do it.

Find out more about Sanskrit. Where was it spoken? Is it still spoken today? What does the Sanskrit alphabet look like?

Terms:

    Sanskrit: an ancient language in which many Sutras are written.

    bronze: a very hard metal made of copper and tin.

    urn: a container

    Dharma Master: a left home person; a bhikshu or bhikshuni

    torrential (rainstorm): a very big storm with lots of water falling in a very short time.

TRAPPED!

Once a hunter went into the deep forest to make a bear trap. He dug up the earth and inserted the trap in the hole; then carefully covered the top of the hole with branches, leaves, and grass. He did such a good job that no human, let alone a bear, would have suspected there was such a trap beneath. After laying the trap he scoured the woods in search of game, taking care to stay far away from the bear trap so animals would not detect a human scent on the snare.

Time passed and he lost his way in the unfamiliar woods. Wandering at random and growing concerned for his own safety and welfare, he suddenly plummetted down into the very bear trap which he himself had constructed! The trap snapped securely onto his leg, biting into his flesh. He was trapped!

At first he called out frantically, but soon realized that he had purposely gone far into the woods, well away from inhabited areas. In pain and dejection, he sat contemplating his fate. He went through many emotional reactions: anger at his own stupidity, fear for his life, desparation, depression, and resignation. Meanwhile, time passed and he got cold and hungry. More time passed and as the pain in his leg increased, so did his cold and hunger. The cold night air soon penetrated to his bones. Unable to get to water, his thirst grew unbearable. As he endured this torture, a new thought occured to him: this is what the bear he had hoped to trap would have gone through! He was forced to take a long, hard look at what kind of karma he had been making as a hunter. Eventually, all feelings of selfish concern for his own well-being vanished. He only had a single thought of true repentance, and from his heart naturally came forth these vows: "I will never again hunt or trap animals, or kill any living creature."

After that thought of true repentance and that sincere vow were made, he suddenly heard the sound of footsteps crushing the underbrush. Fearing it to be an animal but hoping against hope that it might be a person, he decided to call out. His cry for help was instantly answered and he heard the footsteps running toward the spot where he lay trapped. The person helped him out of the trap and took him back to his home. Such was the response to the power of his vow and the sincerity of his shame and remorse.

ANIRUDDHA

When the Buddha was in the world, he had a disciple named Aniruddha. Aniruddha was the son of the Buddha's uncle, the Red Rice King. The name "Aniruddha" means "not poor." He was given this name because of something that happened to him in a former life.

Long ago, during the time of Pusya Buddha, there was a famine. The crops did not grow, and so there was no food to eat. Many people starved to death. In order to stay alive, people had to eat things they didn't usually eat, like grass and roots and leaves.

At that time, there was a Pratyeka Buddha who went out begging for food. But he did not go out every day. He only went out once every two weeks. If no one gave him anything, he would just go without food for those two weeks.

One day he went down the mountain to beg. But no one made any offerings to him, so he had nothing to eat. He was on his way back up the mountain when a poor farmer saw him. (That farmer was Aniruddha in a former life.) The farmer put his palms together and said, "Holy Master, I see that your bowl is empty. Won't you please take my lunch? I am very poor, so my lunch

isn't much. It's just some cheap rice.
But you can have it if you want."

The Pratyeka Buddha saw that the farmer
was very sincere . He accepted the farmer's
offering of rice. As soon as he had eaten
it, he rose up into the air and disappeared.

The farmer stared up into the sky with
his mouth open. "Now, how in the world did
he do THAT?" he said to himself. Just then
he saw a rabbit running toward him. The
farmer was surprised, because rabbits are
usually very shy. He was even more surprised when the rabbit jumped up on his
back. No matter how hard he tried to get
rid of it, the rabbit wouldn't budge. The
farmer couldn't knock it off or brush it
off or shake it off.

He ran home to ask his wife to help
him get rid of the rabbit. By the time he
got home, the rabbit had turned into a
statue made of pure gold. As the farmer's
wife took the statue off her husband's back,
one of the golden legs broke off. Another
golden leg immediately grew in its place.

From that day on, the farmer and his
wife were never poor. Whenever they needed
money, they would break off a piece of the
golden rabbit. Then they would use the
gold to buy whatever they needed. The
statue was never used up, no matter how
many times pieces were taken from it. For

all the rest of that life, and for many
life-times in the future, Aniruddha was
never poor.

"THERE ISN'T ANY" CAKE

Aniruddha was the Buddha's cousin; he was also a prince. He was raised in the splendor of the
royal palace and always had everything he wanted.
He never heard the word "no". One day he was playing marbles with six other princes. In the game,
whoever lost had to provide cake for everybody.
Aniruddha lost, so he sent the servant home for
cake. He lost again and had to supply cakes again.
This went on for several more times. Finally his
mother told the servant, "There isn't any cake to
send." The servant came back and told Aniruddha
what his mother had said. Remember that Aniruddha
had never heard the word "no". So he thought "there
isn't any" was a kind of cake. So he said to the
servant, "Well, then bring 'there isn't any' cake
here."

The servant returned and told Aniruddha's
mother that Aniruddha wanted some "there isn't
any cake". His mother then realized that she'd
never said "no" to him before. "We've never
told him that 'there isn't any' anything. Whatever he has wanted has always been there. So I guess
we'll have to teach him what 'there isn't any'
means."

Aniruddha's mother then took a great big bowl
made of gold and covered it with a plate made of
gold. Inside there wasn't anything. She gave it
to the servant and said, "Here, take this to Aniruddha. This is 'there isn't any' cake."

15

However, in the past, Aniruddha had made an offering to a Pratyekabuddha, who was moved to vow that in the future, Aniruddha would never know the meaning of the words "there isn't any." This means that in every life, Aniruddha would always have whatever he wanted. So now as the servant was carrying the golden bowl covered with the golden platter which had 'there isn't any' cake inside--that is, it had nothing inside-- the ghosts and spirits who were watching saw that Aniruddha was going to have to find out the meaning of the words 'there isn't any.' "We'd better do something!" they said to one another. Immediately they brought a cake from the heavens and put it in the bowl. When the servant got back to Aniruddha with the bowl, he and his royal playmates pulled the plate off of the bowl because they were all excited to see what kind of cake was inside. The aroma of heavenly cake was so wonderful that it filled the whole city. People started coming out of their houses all over the city. They were wondering, "What smells so good? I've never smelled anything as good as that in my whole life."

Of course when the young princes ate the heavenly cake, they found it absolutely delicious.

The cake was so good that when Aniruddha got back home he said to his mother, "Mother, do you love me?"

His mother said "Yes, I love you as much as a person who only has one eye loves that one eye and protects and cherishes it. I love you just that much!"

17

Aniruddha said to his mother, " Well, mother
if you love me, then why is it that until today
you've never given me any of that delicious 'there
isn't any ' cake?"

Aniruddha's mother caught on quickly. She
said to Aniruddha, "Was there cake inside that
bowl I sent you today?"

Aniruddha replied, "Was there cake inside
that bowl! It was filled with the most delicious
cake I've ever eaten in my whole life!"

When his mother heard that, she thought to
herself, "Aniruddha really has a lot of blessings."

Aniruddha said to his mother, "From now on,
I don't want any other kind of cake. I just want
that kind you gave me today--'there isn't any'
cake." So from then on, whenever Aniruddha asked
for "there isn't any" cake, his mother would take
a bowl and put a plate on top of it. She knew
that when Aniruddha opened it, there would be
heavenly cake inside for him to eat.

THE LITTLE SHRAMANA

Once there was a Dharma Master who could know
everything about a person's past lives. He had
a little Shramana disciple who was only eight years
old. One day, the Master entered samadhi, and he
saw that the little boy had only seven days left
to live. He thought, "I should send him back home.
It would be better for him to die at home with his
parents than here in the forest."

18

So the Dharma Master sent the little Shramana back home to be with his parents. Besides, the little boy's mother missed her little son. He had left home when he was really young and she had not seen him for a long time. She often wished he would come back home so she could see him again.

The Dharma Master told the little Shramana, "You can go back home to visit your parents, but come back after ten days."

The little boy was really happy, because he really wanted to see his mom and dad again. He bowed to his Master and set out for home.

On the way home, it began to rain very hard. The little boy saw an ant hole by the side of the road. He could see that in a little while the rainwater would flow down into the hole and drown all the ants. He thought, "My Master told me that disciples of the Buddha should help all living beings. We should be compassionate and protect all living beings." So he used his hands to dig a little moat around the ant hole to keep the rainwater from going in. In that way, the ants didn't drown and their lives were saved.

When he got home, his parents were glad to see their little son. After seven days, the little boy was still alive. Ten days passed, and the little boy was still okay.

Then the little Shramana said good-bye to his mom and dad and returned to the forest where his teacher was. When the Dharma Master saw the little Shramana still alive he thought, "Oh, he has come back. I thought he was already dead. Is this a ghost who has come back?" The Master decided to sit in meditation to see why the little boy was still alive. He saw how the little boy rescued the ants. Saving those ants was a good thing to do.

The Master said to the little Shramana, "You created a lot of merit while you were away."

The little Shramana said, "The whole time I was gone I stayed at my parents' home and did not do any merit."

The teacher replied, "Yes, you did. You saved the lives of some ants. And because of that act of merit, although you were supposed to die in seven days, you didn't die. Now you will live until you are eighty years old."

The little Shramana was really happy, and from then on he really cultivated well. After that he saved the lives of many creatures. Later on he certified to Arhatship.

From this story you can see that if we people can save other living beings, we will have long lives and never get sick.

How the Buddha Helped Little Roadside Remember Two Words

When the Buddha was in the world, there were two brothers. The older brother was very smart. The younger brother was very stupid. His name was Little Roadside. He was so stupid that he forgot everything. He could not even remember three or four words.

His brother tried to teach him a little poem. But Little Roadside could not remember it.

Then 500 Arhats came to help Little Roadside learn the poem. But no matter how hard they tried, Little Roadside could not remember anything. Over and over the Arhats would tell him what to say. Over and over, Little Roadside would forget.

"Say the poem," said the Arhats.

"But I can't remember it!" cried Little Roadside.

At last his brother got angry.

"You are good for nothing!" he shouted. "You are useless! You can't leave home!"

Little Roadside was very unhappy. "If I can't leave home," he shouted, "then I will kill myself!" He ran into his house and got a rope. Then he ran out to the back yard and climbed up into a tree. He was all set to hang himself.

Just then, the Buddha came to see Little Roadside in the tree. But he did not look like the Buddha. He looked like a tree spirit.

The Buddha said, "You don't have to kill yourself. You can cultivate right here. How do you know that you can't leave home? Maybe your brother is wrong."

21

"You may be right," said Little Roadside. "After all, my brother is my brother. He isn't me. He can't tell me what to do."

"That's right," said the Buddha. "Now, since you can't remember four words, I'll give you two words. SWEEP CLEAN. Use these words to sweep your heart clean. Sweep the floor and sweep your heart. Get rid of the dust."

"Oh, good!" said Little Roadside. "I can remember that. Now, let me see. Sweep...what was the other word?"

"Clean," said the Buddha, "Sweep clean."

"Oh yes," said Little Roadside. "Clean... now what was the first word again!"

The Buddha smiled at Little Roadside. "Sweep," he said.

"Sweep clean!" said Little Roadside. "I did it! Sweep clean!"

Little Roadside worked very hard all week. All the time that he was sweeping the floor, he said to himself, "Sweep clean! Sweep clean! I'm sweeping the dust from my heart." Before the week was over, Little Roadside became enlightened.

AFTER YOU READ

1. Why did Little Roadside's brother get angry at him?
2. How did the Buddha help Little Roadside?

Give the meanings for the following words:

stupid
useless
Arhat

23

THE OLD MAN AND THE RED SNAKE CLAN

This is a story that happened in China a long time ago in the Ming Dynasty (1386-1644 A.D.).

Mr. Fan was an elder. Just before his first son was to be born, Mr. Fan bought a plot of land to prepare as an ancestral burial ground in honor of the expected birth of his child.

The night before Mr. Fan was to begin work on the ancestral ground, he dreamed that an old man wearing a red robe came to him and pleaded,

"This has been the home of my clan for a very long time. There are 800 of us living here now. Please give us three days to relocate before you begin preparing the land for your ancestor's graves. If you will wait, I will repay your kindness." He repeated his plea respectfully three times and bowed to the Elder, then he left.

When the Elder Fan awoke, he remembered the dream, but he thought, "That is nonsense. It was just a dream, and I have already planned to start the work today." So he went right ahead with his plans and ordered his workers to clear the new plot and begin the work.

While they were working, the men found an ancient cave, which could be used as a tomb. Inside the cave they found many red snakes, 800 in all. The Elder Fan ordered his workers to burn them all to clear the cave so he could use it to put the bones of his ancestors in.

That night, the Elder dreamed of the old man wearing the red robe again. The old man cried

24

and said bitterly, "You ignored my sincere plea and ordered your men to burn my entire clan to death. Since you have exterminated my whole clan, in the future I will do the same to you.

The Elder Fan lived and died and was reborn next life as an Emperor. And when he passed away in that life, his son, the crown prince, was next in line to become Emperor.

But in the Emperor's court there was an official who was greedy to be the next Emperor. So the official made everybody believe that the crown prince was too young to be the next Emperor. The official was mean and forceful and everybody was afraid he would start a terrible fight if he didn't get his way.

In the Emperor's clan was another high official. From the time this high official was born he was extremely clever. There was also something else unusual about this high official. He was born with a long, sharp, forked tongue. He also was very good at speaking, and he could always win any argument. When this high official heard that the greedy official wanted the Emperor's throne he wasn't afraid. He spoke up against the bad official. The bad official said to him,

"If you dare to go against my wishes, then I will destroy your whole clan. I will wipe out all nine kinds of your relatives, including the crown prince."

The official with the sharp tongue said, "All right, go ahead. I'm not afraid of you."

And so that's just what the bad official did. He ordered all the people of the Emperor's clan killed. There were 800 people in all.

Who do you suppose the high official with the sharp tongue had been in his former life? He was the Elder Snake who said to the Elder Fan, "Please don't kill my family!" The snake was reborn into the Emperor's clan and he caused the ruin of that whole clan. In this way, the emperor had to pay back his murderous debt.

So, you see, cause and effect is never off by a hair's breadth. We have to be careful in everything we do and follow the Buddha's teachings. Everything we do causes other things to happen. You can't just kill a bunch of snakes and think that nothing will happen to you as a result.

When you plant squash seeds, they grow into squash plants. When you plant beans, they grow into bean stalks. When you do bad things, bad things will happen to you. When you do good things, good things will happen.

KING YAMA AND THE MAN WHO ATE MEAT

Once there was a man who ate meat all his life. When he died, he came before King Yama. He was very surprised to see a big crowd of pigs, chickens, sheep, and cows there, too. "What in the world are all these animals doing here?" he said to himself. He found out very quickly.

One of the pigs spoke up and said, "When this man was alive, he ate a pound of pork. That pork came from my body."

A sheep spoke up. "That's nothing! He ate two pounds of lamb. The lamb came from my little baby sheep!"

A chicken said, "Two pounds? Well, he ate three pounds of chicken. In fact, he ate my whole body! Now it's going to be my turn to eat him!"

The man turned to King Yama. He tried to make excuses for himself. He said, "It's not really my fault, you know. The meat was just there in the store, so I bought it. I didn't kill any animals myself." Then he turned to the animals. "You animals should get the man who sold me the meat. He's the one who's really to blame."

Before the man could blink his eyes, the owner of the store where he bought the meat was standing next to him. King Yama said to the store-owner, "You were selling meat. Don't you know that you were doing something bad?"

The store-owner also tried to make excuses for himself. "Yes, I sell meat, but I only do it

because people want to buy it. If people didn't
buy any meat, I certainly wouldn't sell it. It's
not my fault at all, you see."

Then the man who ate the meat spoke up again.
"But if you hadn't sold me the meat, how could I
have eaten it?"

The store-owner said, "Look. It's not my
fault and it's not your fault. I'll tell you who
is to blame. It's the man who killed the animals.
He's the one who really should be here."

Before the two men could blink their eyes, a
third man was standing next to them. He was wearing a bloody apron. He was the butcher who killed
the animals, cut them up, and sold them to the
stores.

King Yama spoke very sternly to him. "Don't
you know that killing animals is a very serious
offense? What do you have to say for yourself?"

The butcher began to make excuses just as the
other two men had done. "I only killed the pigs
and cows and chickens because people wanted to eat
them. If nobody wanted to eat them, I wouldn't
kill them."

What do you think? Who was really to blame?

In the end, King Yama said to the meat-eater,
"There's no getting around it. If you ate pork,
you must be reborn as a pig to pay back the pig.
When you are killed, and someone eats you, you
will have paid him back. You also ate chicken.
Since you did that, you must also be reborn as a

28

chicken so that someone can kill you and eat you. And you ate beef. So you must also be reborn as a cow to repay the cow."

"Wait a minute," said the man who ate meat. "It will take me many life-times to pay back all the animals I have eaten. When will I ever be reborn as a human being again?"

King Yama looked at the man for a minute before he answered. "You should have thought of that before you ever took your first bite of meat!"

THE FOOLISH FARMER OF SUNG

Once long ago, there was a farmer who lived in the country of Sung. This country was part of China. The people who lived in Sung were not very smart. In fact, they were quite stupid! But this farmer was the stupidest one of all.

One day, he planted grain in his field. He went out the next day to see if the seeds had sprouted. But the field was empty. Every day he went out to check on his seeds. Every day he came back home without having seen anything.

At last came the day he had been waiting for. When he went out to his field, he saw that the brown earth was covered with tiny green seedlings. "This is more like it," he said to himself, "I will soon have lots and lots of grain."

But the next day, when he went out to check on his seedlings, he saw that they were still very short. "This will never do," he said. "I must help these plants to grow." So he went around the field. He pulled every plant up about two inches. It took him all day.

When he got home, he was very tired. His son asked, "What's the matter, Father? Why are you so tired?"

"Ah, my son," replied the farmer, "I have had to work very hard today to help my plants to grow."

The son ran off to the field as fast as he could. He wanted to see what his father had done. As he ran, he thought to himself, "My father is very wise. He knows how to make plants grow very

30

well."

But when he got to the field, he saw that all the plants had withered and died. When the foolish farmer had pulled them up to make them taller, he had pulled their roots right out of the ground. Instead of helping his plants to grow, the farmer had killed them. From this story comes the saying, "he pulled up his sprouts to make them grow."

The moral of the story is: let things happen naturally, don't push too hard. If you are too hasty and push too hard, you end up losing everything, as did the farmer of Sung.

HE GAVE HIS LIFE FOR HALF A VERSE

Shakyamuni Buddha was born into the world many times in many different bodies before he was finally born as the prince who became Shakyamuni Buddha. All during these lifetimes, Shakyamuni Buddha was building the foundation for becoming a Buddha in the future. These earlier lifetimes of the Buddha are often referred to as the times when he was "cultivating on the causal ground", because during these lifetimes he was cultivating or developing the causes that would eventually lead to Buddhahood. The story you are about to read is about one of these earlier lives of the Buddha.

31

Once when Shakyamuni Buddha was cultivating on
the causal ground, he was a Bhikshu--that is, a
monk who had left home. One day the Bhikshu met
a rakshasa ghost. This rakshasa ghost ate people. As the Bhikshu approached the ghost, he heard
him speak the following lines of verse:

"Nothing lasts forever,
    Things come then they are gone."

When the Bhikshu heard these lines, he was
very happy. He said to the ghost, "I am delighted
to hear that you are speaking Buddhadharma. But
32

you've left something out. The Buddhas always
speak in four-line verses, and you have only spoken two verses. Please quickly tell me the last
two lines."

The rakshasa ghost stared at the Bhikshu with
his big red eyes, and said, "So, you want to hear
more Dharma do you? Well, I am very hungry, and
I need to eat. I can't speak anymore Dharma until
I have eaten something. Let me eat you, and then
I will speak."

The Bhikshu replied, "But if you eat me before
you speak the rest of that Dharma, I will die without hearing it, and I won't be able to die happy.
Please speak the rest of the verse for me, and
then you can eat me up."

"All right, "said the ghost. "Here's the
last two lines of verse.

"When the coming and going both stop,
That stopping is true joy."

"Now, step up and let me eat you."

"Just a minute," the Bhikshu called. "I
want..."

"Ah ha!" shouted the ghost. "I suspected as
much. You're trying to get out of your end of the
bargain."

"Not at all," the Bhikshu responded. "But if
I die now, no one else will be able to hear this
verse. Just let me carve it in the trunk of
that big tree over there. Then whoever passes by
the tree will be able to read the verse and culti-

33

vate according to it. Then you can eat me."

"Oh, very well, "grumbled the ghost. "I guess
I can wait a bit longer for lunch. Go ahead."

The Bhikshu began to carve the verses on the
tree trunk. When he had finished, the ghost stepped up close to him, ready for his lunch. But
once again, the Bhikshu asked him to wait.

"What for!?" cried the ghost. "You've carved
it into the tree trunk where everyone can read it.
What more do you want?"

The Bhikshu said, "Eventually, the wind and
the rain will erode the surface of the tree trunk,
and the words will disappear. Let me carve the
verse on this rock here, and then you can certainly eat me."

"Very well, " grumbled the ghost. "Go ahead."

The Bhikshu proceeded to carve the verses into
the rock. When he had finished, he sat down in
meditation and closed his eyes, waiting for the
ghost to eat him. Several minutes passed, but
nothing happened. Finally he opened his eyes.
The rakshasa ghost had disappeared! Then the
Bhikshu looked up into the sky and saw that the
ghost was in fact a god who had come to test him.

"Good indeed, good indeed," said the god.
"You were willing to give up your life for the
sake of two lines of Dharma. That is true vigor."

This is the story of how Shakyamuni Buddha
in one of his previous lifetimes, was willing to
sacrifice his life for half a verse.

The Offering of 500 Upper Garments

After the Buddha had entered Nirvana, one of
his foremost disciples, Ananda, was living in a
park in the City of Kosambi. One day, a many
ministers and court officials were strolling in
the park with the King, whose name was Udayana.
Upon hearing that the holy teacher was in the
vicinity, the ministers and court officials
informed the King and requested permission to
hear what the Sage had to say.

The King gave them permission, and they
hurried to Ananda. When Ananda spoke the Dharma
for them they became so delighted that they gave
500 upper garments to the Sangha as an offering.

The officials and ministers were happy and
pleased. They returned to the King and the King
asked them about Ananda. They told the King about
the wonderful Dharma they had heard. They also
told him about their offering of 500 upper garments.

The King was surprised. He joked with the
ministers and court officials and said, "Is Ananda
going into the clothing business?"

Then the King went to see Ananda himself. The
first thing the King asked when he saw Ananda was,
"What will you do with the 500 upper garments?"

Ananda said, "O King, I intend to give them
to five hundred monks whose upper garments are
old and tattered."

"What will you do with the 500 tattered upper
garments when you give them the new ones?" asked
the King.

"We will make bedspreads out of them,"
replied Ananda.

"And what will you do with the 500 bedspreads?"

"We will make pillowcases out of them,"
Andanda answered.

"And what will you do with the five hundred
pillowcases?" asked the King.

"We will make floor mats out of them,"
answered Ananda.

"And what will you do with the 500 floor
mats?" asked the King.

"We will make foot towels out of them,"
replied Ananda.

"And what will you do with the 500 foot
towels?" asked the King.

"We will make cleaning rags out of them,"
answered Ananda.

"And what will you do with the 500 hundred
cleaning rags?" asked the King.

"We will shred them, combine them with mud,
and use them as flooring," answered Ananda.

From this the King could see that monks never
waste anything. They use every item carefully and
make the most out of what they have. The king was
so delighted that he presented Ananda with 500 more
upper garments.

This was the first time that Ananda had ever
received such an offering.

MAHAKATYAYANA

Katyayana means "literary elegance," because this Venerable One was foremost among the Buddha's disciples in the powers of debate and spoke with great elegance and refinement. His name is also interpreted as "fan-cord " because his father died shortly after he was born and his mother wanted to remarry, but the child Katyayana was a tie, like a fan-cord, which prevented her from being able to do so.

One day Katyayana met a person who believed that after you die there is nothing at all and you won't get born again in another body. That person said to Katyayana, "Buddhists believe that after death there is rebirth. If that is true, why hasn't anyone returned to tell about it?"

Katyayana said, "Suppose a criminal were arrested, tried, and given a jail sentence. Would he be free to return home?"

"No," came the reply.

"The beings in the hells are even less free to come and go," said Katyayana.

The non-Buddhist said, "That may be true for those born in the hells, but those born in the heavens are very free. Why haven't any of them ever sent a letter home telling their family where they are?"

Katyayana said, "That's a good question, but suppose someone slipped and fell into a toilet, not a flush toilet--obviously no one could fall into a flush toilet--but into a pit toilet about us big as a room. Once he got out, would he jump back in again?"

"Goodness, no!" exclaimed the non-Buddhist.

"The world where people live," said Katyayana, "is just like a toilet, and birth in the heavens is like getting out of it. That's why no one comes back. Even if they did, there's the time difference to consider. For example, one day and night in the Heaven of the Thirty-three is equal to one hundred years in our world. Born there, it would take a couple of days to find a place to stay and get settled, and by the time one returned on the third day for a visit to the human realm, one's friends would have long been dead."

The man who asked the question couldn't say anything in reply to that answer.

Old Woman Water Carrier

When Shakyamuni Buddha was in India, there
was a little country where he spoke the Dharma. There
he met an old lady, called Don Je Le, who was a
servant and worked for other people. Every day
she had to carry water for people to use.

When the Buddha saw this old lady, he told
Ananda, "Take the Buddha's bowl to the well. There
is an old lady there. Ask her if she can give
some water, and fill the bowl."

When the old lady found out that it was the
Buddha who wanted some water, she was really happy.
She started to take the bowl to the Buddha herself.

Ananda said, "I can give it to the Buddha."

But she wanted to take the bowl herself.
When she saw the Buddha, she was really happy. She
just grabbed the Buddha's feet and bowed.

Ananda said, "The old lady is really impolite.
Why does she act this way?" Ananda did not like
the way she grabbed the Buddha's feet.
But the Buddha said, "listen and I will
tell you. She was my mother 500 lifetimes ago".
That's why she was so happy to see the
Buddha. She was as happy as if she had found some
precious jewels.

Then the Buddha asked the person who the old
lady worked for as a water carrier, "Can you let
her go so she doesn't have to be your servant any
more? Can you allow her to go so she can cultivate?"

Her master said, "Okay." Her master really
believed in the Buddha, so he said, "Sure, sure."

Then Ananda took the old woman to where the nuns were. Mahaprajapati was the leader of the nuns, and she showed the old lady how to shave her head. She helped her leave the home life and become a nun.

After cultivating for a short time, the old lady was certified to Arhatship. Because she was an Arhat, she could see the past and the future.

All the Buddha's disciples wondered how such a lowly old lady could certify to the fruit of Arhatship so fast. They wondered what was the cause of it. They all wanted to know how it could happen.

The Buddha answered, "In the past, when Kashyapa Buddha was in the world, that old woman was an old cultivator who had left the home life. She always cultivated really well and surpassed other people. She worked really hard at her cultivation. Because she had already cultivated in that past life, in this life she was able to become an Arhat fast. When she cultivated in the past she always worked much harder than everyone else. The only trouble was that she became very arrogant. She always looked down on others. She scolded her elders and thought that others didn't match up to her. Since she looked down on others in the past, her retribution in this life is to be a servant who always has to serve other people.

The Buddha continued, "There is also a reason why she is able to see the Buddha in this life. In the past, in India, in a small country named Benares, there lived a mother and her son. They were very poor. The son was deeply filial to his

mother. Every day he went out to work. But the
country they lived in was a poor country, so no
matter how hard he worked he could only make just
enough money to keep him and his mother alive.

"The son said to himself, 'I should go to
another country where I can make more money.' So
the son left for another country. While he was
away, some robbers came to his house and took
everything he and his mother owned. Then they
forced his mother to go away with them and they
sold her as a slave. (Slaves are people who are
taken away from their homes by force and made to
work for other people . The other people say they
own the slaves and never pay them or let them go
free.)

"Some time passed and the son came back with
a lot of money that he had earned. When he heard
the news about his mother, he was very sad. He
looked everywhere for his mother. He was really
filial to his mother. Finally, he found his mother,and
since he had earned a lot of money in the other
country, he was able to buy her back."

The Buddha said, "I was that filial son and
the mother was this old woman water carrier. So
you see if we plant a good seed, in the future we
will reap a good retribution. Everything has a
cause and effect. So in everything we do, we
should not make mistakes."

HOW THE BUDDHA CROSSED OVER
THREE BROTHERS

When the Buddha was in the world, there were
three brothers named Kashyapa. They had a thousand disciples. They were all fire-worshippers,
and they had many powers.

One day the Buddha decided to cross over these
brothers. So he went to the oldest brother's house.
But he didn't want to tell the oldest brother why
he had come. So when Kashyapa opened the door, the
Buddha just said, "I can't go any further tonight.
It has gotten too dark. May I stay here?"

Now, Kashyapa was already one hundred sixty
years old. He was very clever, and he could do
many things. He saw at once that the Buddha was
someone special. But he couldn't figure out why.

"That's strange," he said to himself. "When
I meet someone, I usually know everything about
them all at once. But I can't see what the Buddha
is all about."

Then he said to the Buddha, "Okay. You can
stay here."

But where do you think he put the Buddha? He
put him in the cave where his dragon lived! This
dragon was very fierce. Whenever a person came
into this cave, the dragon would send fire shooting
out of its mouth. The fire would burn the person,
and the person would die.

In the middle of the night, the dragon came
over to where the Buddha was sitting in meditation.
He tried to burn the Buddha. But the Buddha had
entered the Fire-light Samadhi. He could not be
burned.

43

44

45

Then the Buddha used his power to put the dragon into his bowl. He spoke Dharma for the dragon, and the dragon took refuge with the Buddha.

The next morning, Kashyapa was very surprised to see what had happened. He realized that the Buddha had more wisdom and virtue than he did. He wanted to become the Buddha's disciple, so he took refuge with the Buddha. He told all of his disciples to take refuge with the Buddha, too.

When Kashyapa's two younger brothers saw what had happened, they took refuge with the Buddha, too, along with all of their disciples. The three brothers and their one thousand disciples all left home under the Buddha.

AFTER YOU READ

1. Why do you think the Buddha did not want to tell Kashyapa why he had come?

2. Why was Kashyapa puzzled when he first met the Buddha?

3. What convinced Kashyapa that the Buddha should be his teacher?

The three Kashyapa brothers became foremost disciples of the Buddha. Name five other great disciples

Give the meaning for each of the following words:
    samadhi
    meditation
    take refuge

THE JAMBU TREE

In our world called Jambudvipa, there is a tree called the Jambu tree. This tree grows in northern Jambudvipa by the Ni Ni T'o Lo River. It is a beautifully adorned tree with many leaves. It is so exceptionally fine that people really like to see it. It is 100 yojanas, or 900 miles tall. The trunk is 135 miles in circumference. Each branch is 450 miles long. On top of the tree are five especially long branches.

The fruit of the Jambu tree is also quite large. It is delicious and extremely sweet, even sweeter than honey. When the fruit is squeezed, a white juice is produced. If that juice should happen to fall into a river, all the stones in that river turn a beautiful gold color called Jambu gold. If the juice gets on people's hands, their hands turn red.

The fruit on the Eastern side of the tree is eaten by Gandharvas and the fruit on the Western side of the tree is eaten by huge sea creatures. People who are cultivating to become immortals can quickly do so by eating the fruit of the Jambu tree. Moreover, Shramanas who wish to attain the Fourth Fruit of Arhatship can quickly attain that result as soon as they eat the fruit of the Jambu tree.

The roots of the Jambu tree grow in golden sand. This sand is very special. It keeps the tree roots warm in winter and cool and damp in summer.

At the time of the Buddha, there were two
Bhikshus who had heard of the Jambu tree and wanted to go see it. They used their spiritual penetrations to get to the tree. When they got to the
tree, they found that one of the tree's huge fruits
had fallen to the ground. The fruit had split o-
pen when it fell, and it smelled delicious.

One of the Bhikshus decided he'd see how big
the fruit was. He plunged his hand into the fruit.
He stuck it in so far that his whole arm was inside the fruit, all the way up to the elbow, but
he still hadn't reached the pit. That's how big
the fruit was. When he pulled out his arm, it
was all red.

There was another Bhikshu named Long Legs,
who had cultivated very hard in past lives. As
a result, he had spiritual penetrations. He could
walk on water without falling in. He could walk
on grass without leaving a trace. The grass
would remain standing straight up. Long Legs had
heard about the Jambu tree and was eager to see
it. So he went to the Buddha and asked for permission to go to see the tree. The Buddha granted
his request.

Long Legs set out to find the Jambu tree.
He walked and walked, crossing seven mountains
on his way. When he climbed to the top of the
last mountain, he looked all around, but he
couldn't see anything because everything was
black. There was darkness everywhere. Long Legs
was frightened and hurried back to the Buddha.

When he got back to where the Buddha was, people asked him, "Well, did you see the Jambu tree?" Long Legs replied, "I went, but when I got to the top of the mountain, all I could see was darkness. I got scared, so I came back."

The Buddha said, "The darkness you saw was just the trunk of the Jambu tree. It is so big and has so many leaves that it blocked out all the light so that you couldn't see anything."

"In that case," said Long Legs, "I'll go back for another look." This time when he went back and saw the darkness, he didn't get scared. He kept on walking until he got to the Jambu tree, and he went all the way from the south to the north of the tree. He walked past the Ni Ni T'o Lo River. It's water was the cleanest, clearest water that he had ever seen. He thought to himself, "I wonder if my spiritual penetrations will let me walk across this water." But when he stepped out onto the surface of the water, his foot went right down to the bottom. He realized that the water of this river was extremely light. "I wonder if the water from this river would float on top of the water from an ordinary river," he said to himself. He decided to conduct an experiment. First, he took some Ni Ni T'o Lo River water and poured it into an ordinary stream. The pure water floated on top of the ordinary water. Then he tried the opposite. He took some ordinary water and put it in the stream of this very beautiful, light, clear, water, and it sank to the bottom like a rock.

Long Legs felt very happy. He picked a piece
of the fruit of the Jambu tree and took it back
to offer to the Buddha. The Buddha sliced the
fruit and gave everyone a little bit of it to eat.
The juice of the fruit made the Buddha's hand
turn red. He turned to a large boulder next to
him and made a red hand-print on it, and that
hand-print has lasted to this very day.

THE 500 MONKEYS

When the Buddha was in the world, he lived in India. One day he was teaching an Arhat, named Shr Ma, "Go to another grove and build a temple and stupa for people to cultivate and worship in." Then the Buddha gave Shr Ma some of his hair and fingernail clippings to put in the Pagoda, to pray to.

So Shr Ma went away, and when he found the right spot, he built a temple. Then he built a pagoda. After, 500 Arhats came to live in the temple. Everyday the 500 Arhats would light incense and circle around the outside of the temple as they recited. They hung up beautiful banners.

Near the temple were some mountains, where 500 monkeys lived. The monkeys would look down from the mountains and watch the Arhats circle around the new temple.

The monkeys decided they wanted to do what the Arhats did. They wanted to play "Arhat." So they built a little temple with rocks and then they circled around it. They tried to make their little temple look beautiful, just like the one the Arhats had built. But theirs was quite ugly to look at. However, they really liked their little temple. To them it was beautiful. They also hung up banners just like the Arhats had done.

The 500 monkeys would get up early every morning and bow and walk around the temple reciting, just like the Arhats. The monkeys thought it was great fun.

One day a huge storm hit the mountains, causing a tremendous flood. The flood drowned all 500 monkeys at once. But because the monkeys had been

good, they were reborn as gods in the Trayastrimsha Heaven.

They found life in the Trayastrimsha Heaven
most pleasant. As soon as they thought of something good to eat, it would suddenly appear before them.   As soon as they thought of something
pretty to wear, it would suddenly appear for them.
Everything in this heavenly realm was wonderful.
They wondered why they were reborn there.

Gods in the heavens have many spiritual penetrations. One of the former monkeys used his Heavenly Eye to see his past lives. He saw that in
his past life he was a monkey, and that all his
friends were monkeys, too. He saw how as monkeys
he and his friends played "Arhat," and did everything the Arhats did. Then he understood that
playing the game of pretending to be Arhats created enough merit and virtue to cause he and his
friends to be reborn in the Trayastrimsha Heaven!

After the god told his friends what he had
seen, they decided to visit the mountains to build
a shrine in memory of the monkeys. Carrying heavenly flowers and incense, they went down to the
place where they used to play when they were monkeys. There, they built a small shrine, then lit
incense, offered flowers and circled around it.

At that time, there were 500 Brahmins who
lived and cultivated in the same mountains. They
were quite surprised to see 500 beautiful gods and
goddesses descend from the heavens to build a
shrine and offer gifts to dead monkeys.

The Brahmins asked the gods, "Why are you com-

52

ing here to make these offerings? This is really strange!"

The gods told their story to the Brahmins. When they heard it, the Brahmins decided the Buddha-dharma must be wonderful, so they went to learn about it from the Buddha himself.

And so the 500 Brahmins and 500 gods and goddesses together went to see the Buddha on Vulture Peak near the City of Shravasti. Seeing the Buddha, they reverently bowed, knelt down on their right knees and with their palms together, respectfully asked the Buddha their questions. They asked, "What kind of offenses did we create in the past that turned us into monkeys? Why were we drowned?"

The Buddha said, "In the past, you were all Brahmins who cultivated in those mountains. At that time, there was also an Old Shramana cultivating there. The Old Shramana wanted to build a pagoda on the mountain-top, so every day he would climb down from the mountain to fetch water to mix cement. The Old Shramana had cultivated to the point that his body was very light, just like ashes. It was as if he could fly. When the 500 Brahmins saw that the Old Shramana had ability, they got jealous and said, 'Oh, he's just like a monkey.' Then they said to the Old Shramana, 'If you keep going up and down the mountain carrying water all the time, you'll just end up drowning in it!' In this way they tried to scare the Old Shramana so that he wouldn't want to continue his work."

The Buddha said, "At that time, I was that

Old Shramana, and you 500 gods and goddesses were the 500 Brahmins who were cultivating in the mountains. You got jealous of me, and because you called me a monkey and said that I would drown, that is exactly what happened to you."

When the 500 gods and goddesses and the 500 Brahmins all heard this, they understood. The 500 Brahmins said, "Oh, before we didn't believe in cause and effect. We didn't believe that when you plant a bad cause, bad things happen to you, and that when you plant a good cause, good things happen to you. But now we see that everything happens just that way."

Then the Brahmins said, " We have been cultivating bitter practices for many years up in those mountains and we haven't had any success. Now we see that these gods and goddesses were just monkeys who only imitated some Arhats and got to be born in the heavens. So now, we want to leave the home life under the Buddha."

TURTLE STORY

The following story appeared in the newspaper in the 1950's:

A large Navy ship was cruising near a Phillipine boat, when the Phillipine vessel began to sink. As the boat sank, a huge turtle as large as a house suddenly surfaced. It swam underneath one of the survivors of the sunken boat and lifted the man onto its back. The giant turtle then swam over the waves towards the Navy ship while holding the man steady on its shell.

When the turtle reached the Navy ship, it waited until the Navy crew spotted it with their binoculars. The crew also noticed the man sitting on the turtle's back and went to rescue him.

After the man was safely aboard, the giant turtle circled the ship three times. Then facing the ship, the turtle lowered its head and left.

* * *

A VISIT TO POTALA MOUNTAIN

Once there was a mean and unfilial boy. He lived with his mother and was so cruel, when he came home every day from school he would hit his mother, just to let off steam.

His temper was big, nonetheless he heard the name of Kuan Shih Yin Bodhisattva and because of good roots planted in the past, the sound of that name touched his heart.

"Who is Kuan Shih Yin Bodhisattva," he wondered. "I'd like to see her. Does Kuan Yin really

55

have the power to appear in thirty-two bodies? I'd like to go to Potala Mountain and find out for myself," he thought.

Not long after he had this thought, the boy met an old, crippled man who asked to accompany the boy to Potala Mountain. Now that he had a travelling companion, the boy decided to make the journey.

"Good-bye mother," he said. "I'll be spending the night on the island so don't wait up for me."

The old cripple and the young boy then boarded a ferry boat and set off for the island. Reaching their destination, the old man said he was going to visit a monastery and he disappeared, just like that. So now the boy was left alone to look for Kuan Shih Yin Bodhisattva. He walked over mountains and across valleys in search of the Bodhisattva but could find her nowhere. So much walking tired him out; he fell asleep in the grass beside the road.

While sleeping he dreamed the old man came to him and said, "If you want to see Kuan Shih Yin Bodhisattva, return home, she's there now. Kuan Yin will be wearing one shoe backwards and her robe will be inside out," said the old man.

The boy woke up startled and wanted very much to see Kuan Shih Yin Bodhisattva. He decided to quickly return home, and hopped on the first ferry boat, without waiting for his travelling companion.

Reaching his house at midnight he knocked loudly on the door. His mother heard the noise and thought, "Has my son returned? Is he angry with me again?" She rushed to open the door. In her hurry she put one shoe on backwards and threw on her bathrobe inside out. She was dressed exactly the way the old man in the dream said Kuan Shih Yin Bodhisattva would be dressed. She flung open the door.

When he saw his mother, he bowed his head to the ground, his hands outstretched, and said sincerely, with all his heart:

"Homage to the Bodhisattva of Great Compassion; Homage to the Bodhsiattva of Great Compassion; Homage to the Bodhisattva of Great Compassion!"

The boy repeated it over and over as he bowed and bowed to his mother.

"You have been here at home all along. How lucky I am!"

His mother said, "Son, it's me. Why are you bowing when before you used to hit me? Why have you changed?"

The boy said nothing, but suddenly understood that the old man was really Kuan Shih Yin Bodhisattva, responding in a special body to teach him a lesson.

From that day on, he was always kind to his mother. He never fought or hit anybody again. Instead, he did good deeds and helped people.

The Poor Man and the Rich Man

Once there was a very poor man. He wanted to make an offering to the Triple Jewel. But he only had one coin. He used this coin to buy one pint of oil. After he bought the oil, he had no money left at all. Then he took the pint of oil to a monastery. The abbot of the monastery asked th. poor man to have lunch with him.

On the same day, a very rich man came to the monastery. He brought with him many carts. The carts were piled high with big barrels full of oil. The rich man gave 300 barrels of oil as an offering. But the abbot did not even go to see the rich man.

The bhikshus who lived at the monastery were very surprised.

"Why did you ask that poor man to have lunch with you?" they asked. "He only gave one pint of oil. The rich man gave 300 barrels of oil. But you didn't even ask to see him."

The abbot said, "The poor man used his very last coin to buy the pint of oil. It is true that the rich man gave 300 barrels. But he could have given 3,000 barrels just as easily."

The abbot went on, "The poor man did something that was very hard to do. The rich man did something that was easy for him to do. Tell me what you think. Which man has the greater faith?"

CH'EN KUAN'S DREAMS

About 500 years ago, the country of China was at war and hordes of bandits roamed the countryside. There was a most sincere man, Ch'en Kuan, who bowed day and night to Kuan Yin Bodhisattva. One evening in a dream, Kuan Yin Bodhisattva called his name and spoke to him.

"Ch'en Kuan, in a past life you killed a person. In three days that person will come to your home and kill you as repayment. He will be travelling on foot with a gang of bandits. In that gang there will be a fat bandit with a dark face. He is the one who will break down your door and take your life."

When Ch'en Kuan awoke, he remembered the dream and was frightened out of his wits. He knelt before the image of Kuan Yin Bodhisattva and prayed, "Kuan Yin, you came in a dream to describe the person who is coming to kill me. Please tell me what I should do," he pleaded.

That night he had another dream of Kuan Yin Bodhisattva. "Don't be afraid," said Kuan Yin. "Everything that happens to you in life comes from what you've done. If you always sincerely repent of your past wrongs, then there's no need to ever be afraid," said the compassionate Bodhisattva.

"Tomorrow, go to the market and stock up on vegetables, fruits, melons, and tasty treats. When you return home, cook up the best mouth-watering

59

dishes that you can. Make a real feast. Then be ready. The bandits will come in the afternoon about five or six o'clock. When they arrive, you be right there to open the door. Be very friendly and invite them to come in for a meal. The person who wants to kill you is named Wan Dan and he's from He Nan. When he was young, his parents died and so he just joined a gang of bandits because he didn't have anyone to take care of him."

The next morning Ch'en Kuan woke up and remembered the dream. Today was the day the bandits were to arrive, so he bought the food and prepared a fine meal just as Kuan Yin Bodhisattva had instructed. Late in the afternoon, sure enough, there was a violent kick at the front door and a dark-faced man burst in saying, "Where's Ch'en Kuan, I'm going to kill him!" He was blazing with anger.

But Ch'en Kuan replied in his most friendly and sincere manner, "Oh, Come in, come in, Wan Dan!" He used the man's name. "Come and have dinner with me. I have lots of food. I prepared it just for you.

The bandit said, "How come you know my name?"

Ch'en Kuan said, "I've been waiting for you for so long. Come in, I have lots of food for you. I'd like to talk to you. You see, I also know that you are from He Nan and that when you were young, your parents died and you had no choice but to join up with bandits in order to survive."

"How do you know all that about me?!" demanded the bandit.

Then Ch'en Kuan related his dreams to the bandit and told him what Kuan Yin Bodhisattva had said. "In the past, I killed you, so now I owe you my life. Kuan Yin Bodhisattva told me that." Then he knelt down before him and said, "Now you can kill me. Because of cause and effect, that's how it should be."

But Wan Dan the bandit said, "No, no, no. You've been so nice to me I don't want to kill you. If that's really how it is, then if I kill you in this life, maybe next life you will want to kill me again." Now the bandit who had been so angry and ready to kill Ch'en Kuan understood about cause and effect and no longer wanted to kill him. He said, "Let's stop it right here and not kill anymore."

The two men sat down to eat and had a heart to heart talk. Wan Dan told him how miserable the life of a bandit is. Bandits are always running from the police and often get caught and thrown in jail.

"After my parents died, I joined the outlaws so I'd have food, clothes, and a place to sleep. But I never enjoyed robbing and killing people. I'm tired of leading such a wicked life," he said.

Before he met Ch'en Kuan, however, he had never thought to stop his evil ways. Now, after hearing of Ch'en Kuan's dreams of Kuan Yin Bodhisattva, Wan Dan the bandit decided to start all over and become a good person. He left the gang of bandits and found a good occupation. And for the rest of their lives, he and Ch'en Kuan stayed the best of friends.

THE DEER PARK

Once long ago there was a Prince whose palace was surrounded by a beautiful park. There were gardens full of colorful flowers and broad green lawns shaded by tall trees. The park was the home of two large herds of deer. It was a wonderful home for the deer, except for one thing.

The Prince was a meat-eater, and he was especially fond of venison, or deer-meat. Every day he sent his hunters into the park to kill some deer from the herds. Every day the hunters killed six or seven deer. But even though the Prince was fond of venison, he could not eat more than half a deer in one day. As a result, there was a great deal of wasted meat. More deer were killed than were needed to feed the Prince.

The two herds each had a fine, strong buck as their leader. One was white and one was black. They got together to discuss the problem of so many deer being needlessly killed. They decided that

they would go to the Prince and ask him to stop sending out his hunters. Instead, they would promise him that every day a deer would come to the palace and volunteer to be killed. If the Prince agreed, they would be able to save the lives of many deer, because the Prince certainly couldn't eat more than one deer a day.

The two deer went to the palace and asked to see the Prince. Believe it or not, the Prince was not too surprised when his servants came in

and told him that there were two deer who wanted
to speak to him. Although there are many wonderful
things in the world, it is often hard for people
to recognize them. The Prince didn't see anything
unusual in having two talking deer come to see him,
and he asked that they be sent to him.

After listening to what the two deer had to
say, the Prince thought that their proposal was
very reasonable. Together, they resolved that each
day one deer would offer itself to the Prince.
One day the volunteer would come from the white
deer's herd, the next day from the black deer's
herd,and so forth.

When the rest of the deer heard what had been
decided they were very happy. They realized that
the herds would prosper now that the deer were not
going to be killed off as quickly as before. Of
course it was difficult for the volunteer who had
to give up his life on any particular day. But the
volunteers always went willingly, because they
knew that many other lives were being saved because
of their sacrifice.

There came a day when it was the turn of a
doe from the black deer's herd to go to be killed.
But because she was pregnant, and due to give birth
to a fawn in only a few more days, she went to
plead with the black deer. "I don't mind taking
my turn, " she said to him, "but I would like to
wait until after my baby is born. If I am killed
today, my baby will have to die too. Can't you
find some other deer who will go in my place today? I will take my turn willingly as soon as my

baby is born."

The black deer was black for a reason. He
was not very compassionate, and his heart was not
pure. He said, "You must be crazy! Who would be
so foolish as to give up his life to save yours
for only a few days?" But the pregnant doe continued to plead and cry and finally he said, "Well,
I can see you will give me no peace. Go over to
the white deer's herd and see if you can find some
simpleton over there who will be willing to die
for you."

The doe hurried across the park to where the

white deer stood watching over his herd. Without
much hope, she repeated her request. Now, unlike
the black deer, the white deer had a pure and compassionate heart. He looked at her kindly, and
said, "I very much doubt that any of the deer in
my herd would be willing to sacrifice themselves
in order to allow your fawn to be born. After all
everyone likes to live; no one likes to die."
When the doe heard this, her heart sank, and she
sadly started to turn away. But the white deer
had not finished speaking. "You don't have to
worry, I will go to the palace today to be killed
in your place." The doe could hardly believe her
ears. The white deer, who, as leader of the herd,
could easily have avoided being killed for years
and years, was willing to go in place of a young
doe who wasn't even a member of his own herd. She
thanked him over and over again, and then returned
to her herd to await the birth of her fawn.

The white deer went to the palace. When he
arrived the Prince asked, "What in the world are
you doing here?"

The white deer replied, "I've come to provide
your supply of venison for today. It is my turn
to be killed today, just as we agreed."

What do you mean? How can it be your turn?"
asked the Prince. "You are the leader of your
herd. You should certainly be the very last one
to be killed. There must be many other deer who
could have come in your place."

Then the white deer explained how he had come
to save the life of an unborn fawn. As soon as
he heard this, the Prince felt great shame.

66

"You are a deer with a man's head, while I
am a man with a deer's head, " the Prince told
the white deer. "I will never eat meat again."
The Prince had suddenly realized that because
he had eaten so much meat, he was really like an
animal himself. The deer, on the other hand, had
the wisdom and virtue of a great man, even though
he was an animal.

The Prince was as good as his word, and from
that day on, he never again ate meat. The two
herds of deer grew and prospered in the beautiful
park.

And that is the end of the story, except for
one thing. The white deer was Shakyamuni Buddha
in a former life. The black deer was Devadatta,
the cousin of the Buddha and his rival. In many
many lifetimes, they came together and had con-
tests.

THE SHURANGAMA SUTRA:
THE TREASURE OF THE COUNTRY

When the Great Master Jr Je, "Wise One" heard
about the Shurangama Sutra, he was so deeply moved
that he bowed to it, even though it was far away
in India. He faced the West (towards India) and
bowed every day for eighteen years, hoping one day
he might see this Sutra. But in the end, he never
saw it. How lucky we are to be able to read it
and recite it today!

Do you know how we got the Shurangama Sutra?

Nagarjuna ("Dragon Tree") Bodhisattva brought it
back to India from where it was stored in the Dragon King's library beneath the sea. The King of
India proclaimed it a national treasure and for-
bade anyone to take it out of the country.

At that time, a courageous Bhikshu, Dharma
Master Paramiti, wanted everybody to have a chance
to read and recite the <u>Shurangama Sutra</u> , especial-
ly the people in China. But when he tried to car-
ry the Sutra over the border between India and
China, the border guards stopped him. They said,
"The <u>Shurangama Sutra</u> is a treasure of the country.
You cannot let it leave the country! Go back!"
So Dharma Master Paramiti went back. But he did
not give up.

He thought of a plan. "I'll write the Sutra
out in very tiny letters on very fine silk. Then
I'll roll it up and seal it with wax."

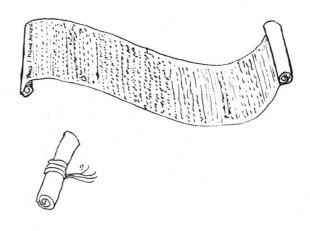

68

Then what do you think he did? He cut open
his arm and put the small scroll inside his flesh.
Then he put medicines on the wound and waited for
it to heal. After the cut healed he tried once
more to cross the border. This time the Sutra
was so well hidden that nobody tried to stop him.
He walked right past the border guards.

The Bhikshu arrived in Canton and quickly
translated the Sutra into Chinese. Then he hurried
back to India because he didn't want the border
guard to be wrongly punished for the crime the
Dharma Master had committed.

He said to the King, "I broke the law on purpose to bring the Shurangama Sutra to the people
of the East. Now I've come back to take whatever
punishment I have coming to me."

Only a great hero would have such courage
and honesty. Now the <u>Shurangama Sutra</u> has come to
America and we can read it in English. How lucky
we are!

"I'M GOING FOR SURE!"

Once there was a monk named Ching Hung. His
job in the temple was to go into the mountains to
gather firewood. All day long while he was col-
lecting firewood, he recited "Namo Amitabha, Namo
Amitabha, Namo Amitabha..." over and over. He did
this for many years.

One cold winter day when he returned to the
temple with a load of firewood, he went to see the
Abbot and said, "I want to leave." But the Abbot

said to him, "It's the middle of the winter session and it is freezing. We need you to gather firewood. If you leave now, everyone will be cold. You can see that it is not a good time for you to leave."

"All right," Ching Hung agreed. "I'll stay until the meditation session is over." When the session was over, he went back to the Abbot and said, "May I leave now?"

"Oh, but it's almost New Year's," said the Abbot. "If you leave now, the people who come here to celebrate New Year's will be cold. Please wait a few more days."

Ching Hung agreed to wait a bit longer. After ten days had passed, he went back to the Abbot and said, "This time, I'm going for sure!"

"All right, fine," said the Abbot.

Then Ching Hung said to the Abbot, "I've lived with all the monks here for a long time. Since we have been together for so long, may I ask some of them to send me off?" The Abbot gave his consent.

The next day at lunch, the Abbot said, "Our monk, the one that always gathers firewood for us, is leaving today. We should all see him off when he leaves. We will all meet in his room at two o'clock this afternoon to send him off. Each of you should wear your robe and sash and dress very properly. Remember to bring the wooden fish and the bell."

When the people who lived at the temple heard this, they were surprised. "That's strange," they said to one another. "He's just an old monk who brings in the wood, why are we doing a special ceremony for him?" But at two o'clock the weino and the rest of the assembly gathered together and they all went to Ching Hung's room.

Ching Hung had cleaned up his room very nicely. There was a table in the room with a Buddha Image on it. As the assembly filed in, they saw Ching Hung bowing to the Buddha. After a few minutes, the Abbot entered the room. He began to recite a poem he had composed for Ching Hung's leaving.

All of a sudden, the other monks realized that the wood-gatherer wasn't just going to leave the monastery. He was _really_ going to leave. He was going to leave this world. He was such a good cultivator that he knew when it was time for him to go and be reborn. He could say, "All right! This is the day I am going."

Everybody sincerely recited the <u>AMITABHA SUTRA</u> and the <u>OFF-TO REBIRTH MANTRA</u>, and then together recited the Buddha's name. The monk Ching Hung sat in the midst of them with his recitation beads in his hand reciting "Namo Amitabha Buddha, Namo Amitabha Buddha." Suddenly his beads dropped to the floor. When everyone looked, he had already gone off to rebirth.

Everyone else continued to recite the Buddha's name very sincerely for one day and one night. Then they all dedicated the merit to living beings and finished the ceremony in honor of the wood-gatherer.

KUAN YIN BODHISATTVA IN A CLAM SHELL

In the T'ang Dynasty in China there was an
emperor who was very fond of clams. But they
couldn't be had year round, so when they were in
season, he would order the people in the kingdom
to hunt for clams for him to eat. The work of
hunting for clams was sometimes dangerous because
of the tides and storms and because the clammers
had to go looking down deep in the water, and so
in the process of looking for clams for the emperor
to eat, many people died.

One day, someone found a super huge clam with
a shell as big around as you can hold in your arms.
He took it back and showed the Emperor his catch.
But when he tried to open it, to get the clam out,
no knife would work to open the huge shell. It

73

像漢羅中蜊蛤

had a big muscle that made it stay shut. However,
all the Emperor had to do was tap the shell with
his finger and it opened. The fellow who had
caught the clam was amazed for he had pried and
pried and couldn't get it open. When the shell
opened up, guess what was inside? It was an image
of Kuan Yin Bodhisattva. That's all there was
inside the big shell, just an image of the Bodhisattva, no clam. In the image there were eighteen Arhats, nine on either side of the Bodhisattva. This image was taken to P'u T'ou Mountain,
the sacred mountain in China dedicated to Kuan
Yin Bodhisattva. And it can still be seen there.

However, the Emperor didn't understand what

74

the image was all about, so he called in a
Chyana Master and asked him to explain it to him.
The Dhyana Master told him, "When Kuan Yin
Bodhisattva wants to cross over beings he appears
in all kinds of forms to do so. And because you
like to eat clams and you make people risk their
lives and even die trying to get them for you,
Kuan Yin Bodhisattva wanted to show you that your
greed for food should not be the cause for other
people's deaths. That's how Kuan Yin Bodhisattva
is trying to teach you this lesson."

So the Emperor, whose name was Wen Chung,
told everyone in the country about the image of
Kuan Yin and issued an edict that every temple in
the whole country should put an image like it
of Kuan Yin and everyone should worship him.
Also, it wasn't just the Emperor who didn't eat
clams anymore. Nobody in the entire country ate
clams after that. And they didn't just stop
eating clams. They never again ate the flesh of
any other animal.

THE DHARMA MASTER AND THE BIRDS

Once there was a Dharma Master in China who was very wise. When he explained Sutras, the gods came down from the heavens to hear him. But no humans ever came to hear him. The Dharma Master knew why people did not come to hear him. It was because he did not have any affinities with them. He decided to do something about it.

He bought some sacks of rice to give to the birds and went up into the mountains to live. Every day, he said the <u>Great Compassion Mantra</u> and the <u>Shurangama Mantra</u> many times. He recited all day and all night, without stopping to rest. He said the mantras over the rice before he gave it to the birds. He hoped that the birds who came to eat this rice would be reborn as people because of the power of the mantras.

The Dharma Master recited mantras and fed the birds in the mountains for twenty years. Then he came back down from the mountains and went into the city again. Once more, he began to explain the Sutras. But now, instead of being empty, his lecture hall was full of people. All of the young people who lived in the city came to hear the Dharma Master speak. They were very happy to hear him explain the Sutras. These young people had been the birds in the mountains when the Dharma Master was there. They had eaten the rice that he had said mantras over. As a result, they had been reborn as people and they had great affinities with the Dharma Master. Now they all came to study the Dharma with him.

BE CAREFUL NEVER TO STEAL FROM YOUR PARENTS

One night a woman had a vivid dream in which
her former daughter who had died came to her and
pleaded, "Please don't kill that sheep for the
dinner party you have planned. That sheep is me,
your daughter. Because I stole from you and father
so much during my life as your daughter, I have to
undergo this suffering of being a sheep. Since I
have such close affinities with you, I happen to
be the sheep you picked to slaughter to eat.
Please don't do it."

The woman remembered the dream when she woke
up. Next morning she took a look at the sheep and
noticed that it looked like the image of her daughter in the dream. The girl had been wearing a
blue bib and had her hair pulled back on her tem-
ples with barretts. The sheep's chest had a
bluish cast and its wool grew in a pattern about
its ears that resembled the hairdo of her daughter.
Disturbed, the woman decided they had better not
kill the sheep. She went into the kitchen, already
bustling with activity in preparation for the day's
feast and told the cook not to kill the sheep.
"But Madame, it's the main course," he replied.
"What will we serve?" She was called away at that
point to attend to some urgent matter regarding
the party arrangements and got so caught up that
she never got back to the cook.

Suspecting that she was just nervous and no-
ticing that she did not provide him with any sub-
stitute for the mutton, the cook went ahead and

killed the sheep and completed the dinner. But
when the guests arrived, no one would touch the
mutton dish. Already distraught that the sheep
had in the end been slaughtered, the woman asked
her guests why they avoided the sheep meat. They
told her that upon arriving, they all had noticed
that the sheep's carcass hanging in the kitchen
looked like a human being, not a sheep, and therefore they dared not touch the meat.

HOW A POOR WOMAN BECAME
LORD OF THE HEAVENS

Every country in the world has a ruler. Some countries have kings or queens, some have emperors, some have presidents, and some have prime ministers. These rulers are in charge of the people in their countries. The gods in the heavens also have a ruler whose name is Shakra. He is known as the Chief among Gods, and also as the Lord of the Heaven of the Thirty-Three.

How did Shakra come to be a ruler in the heavens? In a previous life, Shakra was a woman who was very poor. Although she was poor, her heart was true and pure. One day as she was out searching for food, she came upon a ruined temple. The roof had fallen away and only the walls were standing. She stepped up to the door to look inside and saw a large Buddha image.

"Oh, no!" she cried. "There is no roof to protect this Buddha. All the gold has worn off. This is terrible! If only I had some money, I would rebuild this temple and repair the Buddha Image. But I am so poor. What can I do?"

Now you or I might have given up at that point. After all, to restore the image and rebuild the temple would take thousands of dollars, and this woman didn't have more than a few pennies. But instead of giving up, she made a vow. Somehow, somewhere, she would find a way to rebuild the ruined temple and restore the image.

She set out to find other poor women like herself who were sincere and devoted to the Buddha. Eventually she found thirty-two women who agreed to help her. Slowly, slowly, they saved every penny they could find. They collected wood in the forests and sold it for firewood in the cities. When they begged for food, they kept only enough to keep themselves alive, and sold the rest. Whenever they had saved a few dollars, they used it for repairs. Gradually the temple was restored and the image was re-guilded.

The merit and virtue from their sacrifices was great. The thirty-three women were all reborn in the heavens. The thirty-two helpers each became a heavenly ruler in one of the Thirty-Two heavens. (There are eight of these heavens in each of the four directions--north, south, east, and west--making thirty-two in all.) The women who found the ruined temple and fulfilled her vow to restore it was reborn as Shakra, the ruler of all those heavens. The Heaven of the Thirty-Three, also called the Trayastrimsha Heaven, is located half-way up Mount Sumeru, which is the world-axis of our universe.

Cause And Effect

I. THE ROAD TO VARANASI

Once in India a wealthy jeweller was hurrying
in his carriage along the highway to Varanasi. Pandu was his name. There had been a thunderstorm to
cool the afternoon, and Pandu was congratulating
himself on the excellent weather and on the money
he would make the next day from dealing in jewels.
Looking up for a minute, he noticed a Bhikshu
walking slowly ahead on the side of the road. The
Bhikshu's steps were firm, his back was straight;
there was an air about him of peace and inner
strength. Pandu thought to himself, "If that
Bhikshu is going to Varanasi, I'll ask him if he'll
ride with me. He looks like a saintly man, and I
have heard that the companionship of saintly men
always brings people good luck." He told his burly
slave Mahaduta to rein in the horses.

"Venerable Dharma Master," said Pandu, opening the door to his carriage, "May I offer you transportation to Varanasi?"

"I will travel with you," the Bhikshu replied, "if you understand that I cannot pay you, for I have no possessions in this world. I can only offer the gift of the Buddha Dharma."

"I accept your terms," replied the jeweller, who thought of everything as bargains and deals. And he made room for the Bhikshu in his carriage.

The Bhikshu -- Narada was his name -- spoke as they travelled of the law of cause and effect. "People create their own destinies," he said, "out of what they themselves do. Good deeds naturally bring good fortune, while people who do evil will pay for it sooner or later."

Pandu was pleased with his companion. He liked to hear good common sense, for he was a practical man, and he also had deep good roots in the Dharma, though he did not know it. But he interrupted Narada rudely when the carriage suddenly jolted to a stop in the middle of the roadway.

"What's this?" he called out in irritation to his slave Mahaduta. "We've no time to waste!" Varanasi was still ten miles distant, and the sun was already sinking in the west.

"A stupid farmer's cart in the road," the slave growled from the coachman's seat.

The Bhikshu and the jeweller opened the carriage doors and leaned out to look. There blocking the

highway was a horsecart loaded with rice. Its right
wheel was lying useless in the ditch. The farmer
was sitting beside it struggling to repair a broken
linchpin.

"I can't wait! Push his cart off the road,
Mahaduta!" Pandu shouted. The farmer leapt up to
protest, and Narada turned to Pandu to ask him to
think of some other way, but before either could
say a word Mahaduta had jumped down from his seat,
heaved at the horsecart, and tilted it into the
ditch. Bags of rice slid off into the mud. The
farmer ran yelling up to Mahaduta, but fell silent
when he realized that the tall slave had twice his
strength. Mahaduta raised his fist; there was a
grin on his face, and it was plain to see he would
have enjoyed giving the farmer a beating, if he'd
thought his master had time for it.

As the slave climbed back into his seat and
took up the reins, the Bhikshu stepped down onto
the road. Turning to Pandu, he said:

"I am rested now, and I am in your debt for
the hour's ride you have given me. What better way
could I have to repay you than to help this unfortunate farmer whom you have wronged? By harming him,
you have made sure that some similar harm will come
to you. Perhaps by helping him I can lessen your
debt. Since this farmer was a relative of yours in
a previous life, your karma is tied to his even more
strongly."

The jeweller was astonished. He was not accus-
tomed to being scolded, not even kindly, as the
Bhikshu had done. He was even more taken aback by
the notion that he, Pandu the rich jeweller, could
ever have been related to a rice farmer. "That is
impossible," he said to Narada.

Narada smiled and said, "Sometimes the smartest people are the very ones who do not recognize the basic truths about life. But I will try to protect you against the injury you have done to yourself."

Stung by these words, Pandu raised his hand in signal to his slave to drive on.

Devala, the farmer, had already sat down by the side of the road again to work at repairing his linchpin. Narada nodded to him and began heaving the horsecart out of the ditch. Devala jumped up to assist, but then he saw that the Bhikshu had far more strength than anyone might have expected from a man with his slight frame. The cart was upright again before Devala had crossed the road. "This Bhikshu is a sage for certain," the farmer said to himself. "Invisible Dharma-protecting gods and spirits must be helping him. Maybe he can tell me why my luck has turned for the worse today."

The two men reloaded the bags of rice that Mahaduta had dumped into the ditch, and then as Devala sat down with his linchpin again, he asked, "Venerable Dharma Master, can you tell me why I had to suffer such an injustice today from that arrogant rich man whom I had never seen before? Is there no sense and no fairness in this life?"

Narada answered, "What you suffered today was not really an injustice. It was an exact repayment for an injury you inflicted upon the jeweller in a previous life."

The farmer nodded. "I have heard people say such things before, but I have never known whether to believe them."

"There is nothing so complicated to believe," the Bhikshu said. "What we do is what we become.

By doing good things, a person naturally becomes good, and good things naturally happen to him. The same is true of evil. Evil acts create bad personalities and unfortunate lives. Everything that you have thought, said, and done makes up the kind of person you are and contains the seeds of your future. This is called the law of cause and effect, or the law of karma."

"That may be," Devala cried, "but I am not such a bad person, and look what happened to me today!"

"Isn't it true, though, friend," Narada asked, "that you might have done the same thing to the jeweller today, if he'd been the one who was blocking

the road, and you'd been the one with a bully for a coachman?"

Devala was silenced by the Bhikshu's words. He remembered that, until Narada had come forward to help him, there had been nothing in his mind but thoughts of revenge. He had been wishing angrily just what Narada had said: that he had been the one to overturn the jeweller's cart and that he had driven on proudly while the rich man struggled in the mud. "Yes, Dharma Master," he said. "It is true."

The two men said nothing for a while, until the linchpin was sound again and the wheel remounted on the cart. The farmer was pondering the Bhikshu's words, for he was a man who, though he had no education, was always slowly trying to think through the reasons for things. He said then suddenly, "But this is a terrible thing! Now that the jeweller has harmed me, I will do some harm to the jeweller. Then he will repay me, and then I will come back to repay him, and it will never end!"

"No, it doesn't have to be as you say," Narada said. "People have the power to do good as well as evil. Find a way to answer the proud jeweller with help instead of with harm. Then the cycle will be broken."

Devala nodded doubtfully as he remounted his cart. He believed what the Bhikshu had told him, but he did not see how he would ever have an opportunity to carry out his advice. How could he, a poor farmer, find a way to help a rich businessman? He invited Narada to sit next to him, and he took up the reins.

His horse had not drawn them far, however, when it suddenly shied aside and came to a halt. "A snake on the road!" the farmer cried. But Narada, looking more closely, saw that it was not a snake, but a purse. He stepped down from the cart and picked the purse up. It was heavy with gold.

"I recognize this; it belongs to Pandu, the jeweller," he said. "He had it in his lap in the carriage. It must have dropped out when he opened the door to look at you. Didn't I tell him that his destiny was tied to yours?" He handed the purse to Devala. "Here is your chance to cut the bonds of anger and revenge that tie you to the jeweller. When we reach Varanasi, go to the inn where he is staying and give him his money back. He will excuse himself for his rudeness to you, but tell him that you hold no grudge and that you wish him success. For, let me tell you, you two are much alike, and you will fall or prosper together in accordance with what you do."

Devala did as the Bhikshu instructed him. He had no desire to keep the money. He only wished to be rid of his karmic debt to the jeweler. At nightfall, when they reached Varanasi, he went to the inn where rich men stay and asked to see Pandu.

"Who shall I say wants him?" said the innkeeper, looking scornfully at the farmer's country clothes.

"Tell him a friend has come," Devala said.

In a few minutes, Pandu came into the hall where Devala was waiting. When Pandu saw the farmer standing there and holding out his purse to him, he was struck speechless with amazement, shame, and relief. But after staring for a moment, he suddenly ran out of the room again, shouting, "Stop! Stop the torture!"

Devala had heard groans coming from a room nearby -- he had thought someone must be dying of a fever. But in a moment a tall and burly man stumbled into the hall, his bare back red and black with welts and bruises. It was none other than Mahaduta, the jeweller's slave. A police officer followed him, with a whip in one hand and a nightstick in the other.

Seeing Devala, Mahaduta started with surprise, and then said hoarsely, "My kind master thought I'd stolen that purse. He had me tortured so that I would confess. This is my punishment for hurting you at his bidding." And he stumbled out into the night, without a word to his master.

Pandu watched him go, thinking that he ought to say something to him. But he was too proud to apologize to a slave, especially in front of so many other people.

The jeweller still had not greeted Devala, nor taken back his purse. At that moment, when he was about to speak, a fat man dressed in rich silks bustled into the room, saying loudly, "Ah, Pandu, they told me what was happening. Fortune's wheel turns round and round, does it not? Ten minutes ago it seemed like we were both ruined men, and now all is well again, hmm? Come on, then, take the purse, for heaven's sake, and thank the good fellow."

Pandu took the purse and bowed slightly to the

farmer. "I wronged you, and you have brought me aid
in return. I do not know how to repay you."

"Why, give him a reward, Pandu, what else?" the
fat man boomed. "Give him a reward!"

Bowing to Pandu in his turn, Devala said, "I have
forgiven you and need no reward. If you had not ordered
your slave to overturn my cart, I might never have had
the chance to meet the Venerable Narada and hear his
wise teaching, which has benefitted me more than any
money. I have resolved never to cause harm to any being
again, since I do not want to invite injury in return.
This resolve has made me feel safe and in control of
my life in a way that I have never felt before."

"Narada!" said Pandu. "So he has instructed you!
He instructed me, too, but I'm afraid I didn't listen
well enough. Take this, good man" -- he gave Devala
some gold from his purse -- "and tell me, do you know
where the Venerable Dharma Master is staying in Varanasi?"

"Yes, I have just left him at the monastery near
the West Gate," Devala answered. "In fact, he told
me you might want to see him. He asked me to say that
you may call on him tomorrow afternoon."

Pandu bowed again -- this time a real half-bow
from the waist. "Now I am truly in your debt," he
said. "And I also believe something else he told me.
He said that you and I were relatives in former lives
and that our fates are tied together, for it seems
we have found the same teacher."

The fat man had been listening impatiently. "Yes,
yes, this noble talk is all very well," he cried.
"But let us get down to business!" He turned to Devala
"Let me introduce myself. I am Mallika, the banker,
a friend of the good Pandu here. I have a contract
with the king's steward to deliver the best rice for
the king's table, but three days ago my rival in
business here, wishing to destroy my trade with the
king, bought up all the rice in Varanasi. If I do
not deliver tomorrow, I am ruined. But now, my friend,
you are here, that is the point! Is your rice of
fine grade? Was it harmed by that idiot Mahaduta?
How much is there of it? Is it contracted? Speak!"

Devala, smiling at the banker's eagerness, said,
"I have brought fifteen hundred pounds of   first
grade   rice. Only one bag got a little wet in the
mud. None of it is spoken for, and I was planning
to take it to market in the morning."

"Splendid! Splendid! To market, you say?" Mallika cried, rubbing his hands. "I expect you'll

94

take three times the price that you could get at the market, will you?"

"Yes, I will," Devala said.

"Of course you will," the banker said. Calling for his servants, he had Devala's cart unloaded immediately. He made his generous payment to the farmer in gold, saying to Pandu, as he counted it into Devala's hands, "A man never knows where help will come from when he needs it. One must never lose hope, for life is indeed a wonderful mystery, isn't it? -- There you are, my good sir!" he said to Devala. "Don't gamble it away!" And he went laughing back to his dinner.

But Devala had no intention of gambling it away. He had already resolved to go to the monastery where the Venerable Narada lived and make an offering of half his profit to the Triple Jewel. The rest he took home and spent carefully as he needed it. From that day he always prospered. The people of his village naturally came to consider him their leader, because of his honesty and wisdom.

The next afternoon, Pandu went to the monastery near the West Gate. Narada received him in the guest hall. Having heard the jeweller's account of what had happened at the inn, the Bhikshu said,

"You still have many doubts, and so I would prefer not to give you all the explanation that you ask for. You will not accept it. Your faith is not yet as deep as the farmer Devala's, and you still have more experiences to undergo before you become a true disciple of the Buddha. But I will give you this advice. Treat all living creatures as you would wish to be treated yourself. Think of every man as your own father and of every woman as your own mother. Remember that your every action, for good or for evil, no matter how small, will be returned upon you in the exact amount, sooner or later. Therefore there is a simple saying: 'If you plant beans, you harvest beans; if you plant melons, you harvest melons. Good brings about good, and evil is repaid with evil'."

"Venerable Dharma Master," said Pandu, who had been listening with close attention, "I beg you to give me the explanation you spoke of, so that I will be better able to follow your wise advice."

"Very well," the Bhikshu said. "Then remember what I say and contemplate it well. In the future you may come to understand. I have told you that we ourselves, each one of us, make our own destinies, in accordance with what we do. Your rich friend Mallika, for example, has many blessings, though little wisdom. He believes that the wheel of fortune, as he calls it, turns round and round mysteriously. But there is no mystery. His prosperity and contented outlook have nothing to do with any force outside of his own actions, thoughts, and words. He is contented and rich, life after life, simply because he is kind and generous, life after life. I do not think he would have treated a slave the way you treated your slave Mahaduta."

"Indeed," Pandu said, "He tried to restrain me. But I was angry and did not listen."

"Yes," Narada said, nodding. "And do not think that you are free of the debt you owe Mahaduta for having had him so cruelly beaten without cause. Do not think that you are alone in this world and that what you do has no consequences. Your fundamental mistake is the same mistake that everyone makes until they encounter the teachings of the Buddha: you believe that you have a separate self. But your self is simply a habit of thought. It is not real. In truth you are of the same basic substance as all other living beings, and so you are more closely related to them in every thought and act than the organs of your body are related to each other. What you think of as your self is nothing but an illusion, a false idea, and the body you cherish is a mere accumulation of the four elements, which will be scattered to the winds upon your death. What endures is your storehouse-consciousness. When your storehouse-consciousness is cleansed of the seeds of evil that you have planted in it, it will return to its original purity. Then you will know for yourself your original identity with all beings.

"If you can truly understand this in your heart," Narada continued, "you will have no more desire to harm other beings, because you will know that they are the same as yourself. You will feel their sufferings as your own. Therefore you will only try to help them. This is the Buddha's teaching of kindness and compassion. Even if, in a moment when your patience is exhausted, you should want to harm someone, you will not dare to do it, because you will know that the harm you do will be returned to you sooner or later. This is the Buddha's teaching of cause and effect. Let this verse be your guide:

He who hurts others hurts himself.
He who helps others helps himself more.
To find the pure Way, the Path of Light,
Let go of the falsehood that you have a self.

Pandu asked the Bhikshu to recite the verse a second time, and he wrote it down in his expense-book and put it in his purse. "I don't intend to forget your words, Dharma Master. Stopping my carriage and offering you a ride on the highway yesterday was the most intelligent thing I have done in a long time. All of us have gained great benefit, both in our fortunes and in our hearts. If everyone understood the teachings of karma and of kindness that you have given us, how much more peaceful the world would be! How much more prosperous and happy the people would be!"

Narada smiled. "Among all the teachings of mankind, none compares to the Buddhadharma   It is wonderful in the beginning, wonderful in the middle, and wonderful in the end. It is wonderful in its principles and wonderful in   application to the life of man. Its teaching of compassion leads people to transcend the self and live in goodness and wisdom."

Pandu rose and bowed down three times to the Dharma Master -- something he had never before in his life done even once to anyone. Then he said, "I now intend to see to the establishment of a monastery in my native place, Kaushambi, so that the people of that town will have the opportunity to hear the wonderful Dharma. I only hope that the Dharma Master will have compassion on me and help me to fulfill this vow."

II. The Robber Chieftain

Years passed, and Pandu the jeweller prospered. The monastery at Kaushambi, because of its association with the Venerable Narada, became widely known as a place of study and cultivation of the Proper Dharma. Pandu became a refuge-disciple of Narada, and he continued to be a leading donor and protector of the monastery he had helped Narada to found. Whenever the press of business allowed, he went to listen to Sutra-lectures given by the Bhikshu Panthaka, who was leader of the assembly at the monastery and a room-entering disciple of Narada. Above

all, Pandu looked forward to receiving the wise instructions of his teacher whenever the Elder Master
visited the town. But he did not become a real cultivator of the teachings himself. He did not practice meditation or recite the Buddha's name. Ceremonies of bowing in repentance for past errors, to
eradicate evil karma, were held regularly at the
monastery, but Pandu did not attend them. He told
himself that these things were the duties of monks,
and that his own worldly business kept him too busy.
     One day, six or seven years after his first
meeting with the Venerable Narada on the road to
Varanasi, an unusual order came to Pandu's workshop.
The king of the neighboring country across the
mountains desired a new royal crown. He had heard
of the beauty of Pandu's jewelwork. The crown was
to be wrought in gold and set about with the costli-
est gems to be found in all of India. Indian kings
had always had a weakness for precious stones, and
Pandu had often dreamed of becoming the supplier of
jewelry to a royal house. Then he would be assured
not simply of prosperity, but of great riches.
Now his chance had arrived.
     Pandu immediately sent out orders for the finest
sapphires, rubies, and diamonds that could be had.
He invested the greater part of his wealth in them.
He designed and worked the crown himself. Then gather
ing together a strong escort of armed men, to ensure
his safety against robbers in the mountains, he set
out for the neighboring kingdom.
     All was well until they reached a narrow pass
at the mountains' summit. There, with a great chorus
of fierce yells, a troop of brigands descended from
the heights. Pandu's escort was greater in number,
but the shying horses and steep sides of the
mountain pass hampered the defenders in battle. In
a matter of minutes Pandu's men were disarmed. Two
unshaven and dirty men threw open the door to the
jeweller's carriage, pulled him out flung him to
the ground, and began kicking him and beating him
with sticks. Pandu bore the blows, thinking only of
his purse, which he clutched against his chest,
concealed in his robes. In it lay the crown and a
store of other jewels with which he had planned to
tempt the king's daughter and the queen.
     "Stop a moment, my boys!" a voice called out
-- a voice that Pandu had heard before, though at
first he could not place whose it was.
     "Stop beating him, I told you!"
     Pandu opened his eyes. There standing

98

over him, dressed in leather clothing, his long hair
bound in a kerchief of red silk, was Mahaduta, the
slave he'd had tortured years before. Pandu had heard
that the greatest of the robber chieftains in the
mountains was a former slave from Kaushambi. But
it had never occurred to him that the slave had been
his own.

"See what he has there in his right hand," Mahaduta ordered quietly.

One of the men who had been beating him planted
his knee in Pandu's stomach, while the other pulled
Pandu's arm away from his chest by slow force. The
jeweller's purse was pried from his hand.

"I'll take that," Mahaduta said. "I have paid
for it already." He took it and put it inside his
jacket. "Have I not, master?" he asked Pandu, in
a voice that was half scorn and half bitterness.

"Shall we finish him, then?" one of the robbers
asked the chieftain.

Mahaduta looked down at Pandu, and he saw in
Pandu's eyes not anger, or fright, which might
have enraged him in turn, but sadness and resignation. He could not know that Pandu was remembering
the Venerable Narada's voice saying, as clearly as
if he'd heard it yesterday: *"Do not think that you are
free of the debt you owe Mahaduta for having him so cruelly
beaten without cause. Do not think that you are all alone in
this world and that what you do has no consequences. If you
can truly understand this in your heart, you will have no
more desire to harm other beings, because you will know that
they are the same as yourself. You will feel their sufferings
as your own."*

Pandu sighed. He suddenly understood that he
had never accepted his teacher's instructions. He
had never truly believed that they applied to him
as well as to other people. They were not simply
logical theories. They were real, and he could not
escape their truth. If he was to die now, violently
and before his time, with no chance to say farewell
to his family, it was his own doing. He had set up
the conditions for it. It was his own fault.

He had never given a thought to what had happened to his runaway slave Mahaduta. The man's suffering in the mountains, especially in winter, and
the desperation and danger of the evil calling that
he, Pandu, had pushed Mahaduta into -- these things
he had never regretted for a moment. Now the time
of payment had come. He coughed and said hoarsely
to Mahaduta, "It is true. You have paid." He

looked away from Mahaduta and waited for the next
blow.

Mahaduta told his men: "Let the jeweller lie.
There is a false bottom to his carriage, underneath the coachman's seat. Knock it loose and take
out the chest of gold pieces that will certainly be
there. We will divide it equally. This is a great
day for all of you."

The men jumped up eagerly. But Mahaduta himself
felt little joy at his revenge, though he had spent
many a cold morning fervently wishing for it. Now
that it had come, he felt heaviness and regret, as
if he were hurting a member of his own family. He
went among his men, telling them to stop beating
Pandu's escort. "Spoils only," he said. "No killing."
And he distracted them with news of the chest of
gold which was, indeed, wedged behind the false
bottom of the carriage, just where Mahaduta himself
had hidden it many times in past years.

The robber chieftain let Pandu and his men go
free down the mountain back to Kaushambi. That evening, when his confederates were counting gold and
rejoicing, he hid the purse in a crevice in his
cave. He did not take it out to look at it again for
a long time.

Pandu was no longer a rich man. He had lost
much of his capital, and without capital a jeweller
can do little. But he blamed no one for his losses
but himself. "In my younger years I was very hard
on people," he told his family. "What has happened
now is simply the payment for my harshness and
arrogance." Bowing in repentance now came very
naturally to him, and he took to reciting the
name of Avalokiteshvara Bodhisattva whenever his
mind was not occupied with conversation or business.
He slowly realized that, at the bottom of his heart,
he was happier now than he had been when he was
rich. His only regret was that he was no longer
able to make nearly so many offerings to adorn the
monastery and support the Dharma, or to help the
poor of the town -- something he had never thought
to do much before.

Again the years passed. Then one day Panthaka,
now abbot of the monastery at Kaushambi, was set
upon by Mahaduta's robber band while walking alone
on a pilgrimage across the mountains. Panthaka
carried no money, and so Mahaduta beat him briefly
and let him go. Panthaka went no further that day.
The next morning, before he had walked far, he heard
the sounds of men fighting just off the road. One

man was roaring in pain. Panthaka hurried to the
scene, hoping to dissuade the robbers from beating
yet another traveller. But instead of an innocent
traveller, it was Mahaduta himself who was being
attacked. He stood in the midst of a dozen of his
own men like a lion cornered by hounds. His great
stick felled several of the other robbers, but at
last he himself fell. He was beaten by his own
stick until he lay as if dead.

Panthaka stayed hidden till the robbers had
left the place. Then he knelt down among the fallen men, only to find that all were dead but Mahaduta himself, and in him there was little life left.
Panthaka walked down to the stream that ran among
the rocks nearby. He filled his bowl with fresh
water and brought it to the dying man,

Mahaduta drank a little and opened his eyes.
He groaned and cried out, "Where are those rotten
thieves that I have led to victory time after
time? They'd have been hanged long ago if it wasn't
for me!"

"Calm yourself," Panthaka said, "and don't
think of your comrades, or of the evil road you
have taken together. Think of your own fate and
of the chance you have been given to repent.
Drink this water, and let me dress your wounds.
Perhaps I may still save your life."

Mahaduta looked clearly at Panthaka for the
first time. "You are the monk who I gave a beating
to only yesterday! And now you have come to save
my life. You shame me." He drank more water and
looked around him as he lay. "Three of them there,
are they dead? And the others have run off, the
ungrateful hounds! I was the one who taught them
to fight, and now they have turned on me."

"You taught them to fight," Panthaka said,
"and they have repaid you by fighting. If you had
taught them kindness, they would have repaid you
with kindness. You have brought in a harvest that
you planted yourself."

"What you say is true. I've often been afraid
they would turn on me -- ah! ah!" He groaned as
Panthaka lifted his shoulder. "I do not think you
can save my life. Tell me, if you can, how I can
be saved from the pains of the hells, which I know
I deserve as payment for my evil life. Lately I
have felt that my death must not be far off, and
the dread of what will come after has weighed like
a heavy stone on my chest, so that sometimes I've
hardly been able to breathe."

"Repent of your offenses and reform with true sincerity," Panthaka said. "Root out the greed and anger from your heart, and fill your heart instead with thoughts of kindness for all beings."

"Alas, I know nothing of kindness," Mahaduta said. "My life has been a story of much evil and no good. I will go to the hells and never escape along the noble Path that you have walked, Dharma Master!"

"Do not despair," Panthaka answered, "and do not underestimate the power of repentance and reform. It is said that a single thought of repentance, if it truly comes from the heart, can wipe away ten thousand kalpas' worth of evil. For example, do you know of the great robber Kandata, who died without repentance and who fell into the Unending Hells? When he had been suffering tortures there for several kalpas, the Buddha Shakyamuni, our Teacher in this age, appeared in the world and beneath the Bodhi Tree accomplished enlightenment. The rays of light that shone forth from between his brows penetrated to the hells and inspired the beings there with new life and hope. Looking up, Kandata saw the Buddha seated in meditation beneath the Bodhi Tree, and he cried out, 'Save me, save me, World Honored One! I am suffering here for the evils I have done, and I cannot get out! Help me walk that Path you have walked, World Honored One!'

"The Buddha looked down and saw Kandata there. 'I will guide you in your escape,' he said to him, 'but it must be with the help of your own good karma. What good did you do, Kandata, when you were in the world of men?'

"Kandata remained silent, for he had been a cruel man. But the World Honored One, with his Buddha-Eye, contemplated the seeds in Kandata's storehouse-consciousness. He saw that once when Kandata was walking on a forest path, he had stepped aside to avoid crushing a spider beneath his feet, thinking: 'The spider hasn't hurt anyone. Why should I step on him?' Seeing this, the Buddha sent a spider to spin a thread of gossamer down to the Unintermittent Hell.

"'Take hold of my thread,' the spider said, 'and climb up.'

"Kandata eagerly took the gossamer and pulled himself up. The gossamer held fast. He climbed quickly, higher and higher. Suddenly he noticed that the spider's thread was trembling, as if under

a new weight. Kandata looked down. He saw that other hell-beings had grasped hold of the thread and were climbing up after him. The thread stretched out, but did not break. Kandata was afraid. More and more hell-beings were taking hold of the thread. Kandata was no longer looking up at the Buddha; he was looking down at the hell-beings following him. He stopped climbing. 'How can the gossamer carry everyone?' he thought. 'The cobweb is mine!' he shouted below. 'Let go, all of you! Let go! It's mine!' Immediately the cobweb broke. Kandata and all the others fell back into the hells.

"Kandata's repentance was not true," Panthaka said to Mahaduta. "He did not reform. The spider's gossamer would have held, for even one generous thought has the strength to be a lifeline that saves thousands. But Kandata destroyed the gossamer. He still held onto the illusion of self, and his evil habits were too strong. He was not willing to help anyone else. Even the World Honored One could not save him."

"Let me think and find that thread of gossamer!" cried Mahaduta. "If there is some good I can do, I will not try to keep it to myself."

The two men were silent for a while. Panthaka washed Mahaduta's wounds. The robber-chieftain breathed more peacefully. Finally he said, "There is one 'good' thing that I did once -- if you can call it good to stop from doing more evil" --

"You can," said Panthaka.

"Yes, and one good thing I still can do. By any chance do you know Pandu, the rich jeweller from Kaushambi?"

"I am from Kaushambi, and I know him well," Panthaka said, "though he is no longer rich."

"Isn't he? I am sorry. Strange: you'd think I'd be glad, for he was the one who taught me to be high-handed with people and to oppress them. When I was a young slave, he sent me to study with a wrestler to learn to fight, so that I could be his bodyguard. Whenever I bullied people, he rewarded me. His heart was as hard as flint. He had me tortured once. It was then I ran away to the mountains. But people have told me that he has changed, and that he is known far and wide for his kindness and benevolence! It is hard to conceive of that. Is it true, Dharma Master?"

"It is true," Panthaka said. "The power of sincere repentance is indeed inconceivable. Every time I see it, it amazes me anew."

"I plotted many times how I would have my revenge on that man," Mahaduta continued. "I intended
to torture him, just as he had me tortured. And he
did fall into my hands at last. But when I saw his
face as he lay there on the road, clutching his
jewels to his chest, resigned to his death -- I
could not do it, Dharma Master. I felt as if I would
be torturing my own brother."

"All men are brothers," Panthaka said. "Every
man has been your father in some life past, and
every woman your mother. And with this man you have
affinities that are especially strong, both for
good and for evil."

Mahaduta nodded. "It must be so. I took his
jewels and his gold that day, but I let him and
all his bodyguards go. His gold I gave to my men,
so they would not care about my calling off the
violence. But his jewels I have with me still,
hidden in a crevice in my cave. For some reason
I could not part with them. It wasn't only that a
crown like that would be hard to dispose of. I also
felt that I had to save them for something -- I
didn't know for what. Now I am glad." Mahaduta
paused a moment, then turned to Panthaka. "Do this
for me, Dharma Master. My cave is behind a tall
cedar by the stream a half-mile above us -- you
can see the broad top of the cedar from the road.
Pandu's crown and his jewels are in the vertical
crevice just to the left of the entrance. You
must reach straight in, then up to the right.
Can you remember that?"

"I can remember."

"Don't go there yourself. Tell Pandu to come
with thirty armed men. My men are fewer now, and
they will lose heart without me. Pandu will over-
come them easily. Tell Pandu I am sorry. I wish him
wealth again. I wish all men wealth and happiness
-- all the wealth and happiness that I have taken
from them. If I live, or in my next life, I vow to
be like you, Venerable Dharma Master, and be a help-
er of men caught in the web of sorrow they have
created by their own foolish deeds."

Mahaduta fell back exhausted. He now felt no
pain from his wounds, but his life was ebbing away.
Suddenly a joyous smile swept into his face. He
raised his hand, pointing gently. "See! The Buddha
on his couch, about to enter Nirvana. His disciples
the Great Arhats are standing around him. See! He
is smiling at me!" And Mahaduta's face was bright
with happiness. "What a wonderful blessing to

106

us that he came into the world!"

"Yes, it was a blessing," Panthaka said. "He appeared in the world out of compassion for living beings, in order to instruct us in the one great matter: the problem of birth and death. He taught us to awaken to the suffering of this world, and he taught us that selfish desire is the source of our suffering. He taught us how to end our suffering by following him on the Proper Path. He taught us morality, concentration, and wisdom to put our greed, anger, and stupidity to rest. He himself, through lifetimes of cultivation and renunciation, put to rest all his own desires, and with kindness, compassion, joy, and giving he came to give us himself as an example. If all men and women could take refuge in him, this world would no longer be the poor and dangerous place that it is now."

Mahaduta nodded. He drank in the Bhikshu's words like a thirsty man who is given cool water. He tried to speak, but could not. Understanding his request, Panthaka spoke the Three Refuges for him, so that he became a disciple of the Triple Jewel. Panthaka then repeated for him the Four Great Vows of the Bodhisattva:

> *Living beings are boundless: I vow to save them.*
> *Afflictions are endless: I vow to cut them off.*
> *Dharma-Doors are countless: I vow to study them.*
> *The Buddhas' Way is unsurpassed: I vow to achieve it.*

He repeated three times the Verse of Repentance of Universal Worthy Bodhisattva:

> *Of all bad karma I have done in the past,*
> *Caused by beginningless greed, anger, and stupidity*
> *And produced by body, mouth, and mind,*
> *I now repent and reform.*

And this verse:

> *Offenses arise from the mind; it is the mind*
>   *that repents.*
> *When the mind is extinguished, offenses*
>   *are forgotten.*
> *Offenses extinguished and the mind*
>   *forgotten -- both empty:*
> *That is what is called true repentance*
>   *and reform.*

As Panthaka was reciting it, Mahaduta breathed his last. He died with a smile on his face.

Panthaka postponed his pilgrimage and returned
to Kaushambi. He went immediately to Pandu's house
to tell him what had happened. Gathering an escort
of armed men, Pandu returned to the mountains. Mahaduta's men had already fled. Pandu's purse was
hidden just as Mahaduta had described, and the crown
was within it, unharmed.

Panthaka came with them, and when Mahaduta's
and his fallen men's bodies had been burned and tne
ashes collected in urns, Panthaka led the assembled
company in the recitation of *The Buddha Speaks of Amitabha Sutra* and the Mantra for Rebirth in the Pure
Land. He spoke briefly of the power of karma and of
the even greater power of repentance and reform.
He quoted this verse from the *Dhammapada:*

> *No one can save us but ourselves.*
> *Our strength is greater than the strength*
>   *we derive from others.*
> *We ourselves must walk the Road to Proper*
>   *Enlightenment*
> *With the Buddha as our Great Teacher and Guide.*

"Our Elder Master Narada," Panthaka continued, "has
always stressed that we alone are responsible for
our own actions, and that we are responsible for
what happens to us as a result of our actions. It
is not the Great God Indra, or Brahma, or any other
being who rewards and punishes us. We reward ourselve
and we punish ourselves. Everything comes forth
from the mind. The world is exactly how we create
it. This man Mahaduta, whom we have buried today,
led an evil life, guided by evil thoughts, and he
knew nothing but unhappiness. But at the end he
changed. His repentance and vows of reform moved
the Buddha himself to appear to him and give him
his blessing. He ended his life with a deed of for-
giveness, and he died in happiness. We can all
learn from his example, for none of us is blame-
less. We are all connected by the web of karma
we have created, and we are all capable of the
liberation that true repentance brings."

On Mahaduta's headstone Panthaka had in-
scribed this summary of the robber-chieftain's
life and conversion:

> *Here lies Mahaduta, highwayman.*
> *He lived in anger; anger felled him.*
> *At last repenting, he returned his spoils,*
> *Promising to walk the Proper Path.*

108

The Buddha smiled and certified his change.
Maha Prajna Paramita!

The headstone beside the mountain pass became known as the Repentant Robber's Tomb, and in later years a shrine was built beside it. There travellers and pilgrims bowed to the Buddha and prayed for a peaceful journey and the conversion of evil men.

Pandu now became wealthy again, wealthier than he had ever been. Now, however, his interest was more in giving money away than in making it, and he gave over the operation of his business to his sons. He did his best to teach them that prosperity brought about by hard dealings will not last, and that by being generous and kind they would assure themselves of a happy future. His end came peacefully in old age. When he realized that his death was near, he called his sons, daughters, and grandchildren to his bedside and told them:

"My dear children, if in the future something should go wrong in your lives, do not blame others, even if they seem to be the cause. Look within yourselves. See where you have been proud, selfish, greedy, or unkind. Change that fault in yourself, for this is something that is always within your power. If change seems beyond you, seek help from your teacher, and pray to the Buddhas and Bodhisattvas for aid. Once you have changed your fault, good fortune and happiness will return to you naturally. When they have returned, do not hoard them, but share them with others. Then they will never be exhausted. Remember me by this verse, which the Venerable Narada taught me when I first knew him:

> *He who hurts others hurts himself.*
> *He who helps others helps himself more.*
> *To find the pure Way, the Path of Light,*
> *Let go of the falsehood that you have a self.*

TRIPITAKA MASTER HSUAN TSANG OF
THE T'ANG DYNASTY

Tripitaka Master Hsuan Tsang's contributions
to Buddhism have been exceptionally great. It can
be said that from ancient times to the present,
there has never been anyone who can compare to
this Dharma Master in his achievements. His worldly
surname was Ch'a. His father was an official, but
a poor one. Why did he end up a poor official? It
was because he did not take bribes. He was not
after the citizens' money or that of the government. He was not like people of these days who
hold office and always feel they are earning too
little money so that on top of their government
salary they force the citizens to give them their
hard-earned money as well. Dharma Master Hsuan
Tsang's father did not want money. He remained a
poor official all his life. Even though he was
poor, he had a virtuous nature and because of that
he had two sons who left the home-life, lectured
Sutras, and were adept cultivators of the Way.

Dharma Master Hsuan Tsang left the home-life
at the age of thirteen and commenced his study of
the Buddhadharma. During those early years of
study, if there was a Dharma Master lecturing a
Buddhist text, no matter who the Dharma Master was
or how far away the lecture was being held, he was
sure to go to listen, whether it was a Sutra lecture,
a Shastra lecture, or a Vinaya lecture. He went to
listen to them all. Wind and rain could not keep
him away from lectures on the Tripitaka, to the
point that he even forgot to be hungry. He just
ate the Dharma, taking the Buddhadharma as his food

Tripitaka Master Hsuan Tsang

and drink. He did this for five years and then
took the Complete Precepts.

However, the principles lectured by the Dharma
Masters he heard were all different. They all explained the same Sutras in very different ways --
each with his own interpretation. And there was
a big difference between the lectures of those with
wisdom and those without wisdom. But Dharma Master
Hsuan Tsang had not yet really opened enlightenment
and he did not have the Selective Dharma Eye, so
how could he know whose lectures to rely on? At
that time he vowed to go to India, saying,

> The Buddhadharma has been transmitted
> from India, and so there is certainly true
> and genuine Buddhadharma to be found in
> India.

Thereupon, he wrote a request for permission to go
to India to seek the Dharma and presented it to the
Emperor. The Emperor T'ai Tsung of T'ang did not
grant his wish, but Dharma Master Hsuan Tsang, who
had already vowed to go, said, "I would prefer to
disobey the Son of Heaven and have my head cut off
than not to go and seek the Dharma." So he returned
to the monastery and began to practice mountain-
climbing. He piled chairs, tables, and benches
together to simulate a mountain and practiced
jumping from one piece of furniture to the next.
This was his method of practicing mountain-climbing.
From morning 'til night he leaped from table to
chair. Probably there were not any big mountains
where he lived, so he had to practice in the temple.
All the young, old and older novices wondered what
he was up to, jumping on furniture all day long
instead of reciting Sutras or cultivating. He did
not tell anyone that he was training to climb the

Himalayas, so most people thought he was goofing off. Eventually, he trained his body so that it was very strong, and then when he was physically able, he started his trip through Siberia.

On the day of his departure, when the Emperor T'ai Tsung learned he intended to go even without Imperial consent, the Emperor asked him, "I have not given you permission and you still insist on going. When will you be back?"

Dharma Master Hsuan Tsang replied, "Look at this pine tree. The needles are pointing toward the west. Wait until those needles turn around and face east. That is the time when I will return." He did not say how many years that would be. So he set out. At that time there were no airplanes, steamboats, buses, or trains. There were boats, but they were made of wood and not too sturdy. Besides, since he did not have Imperial permission, he probably could not have gotten the use of a boat anyway. So he traveled by land through many countries, from the Siberian area of the Russian border to India. He was gone for more than a decade. When he reached India, he did not know the language at all. But bit-by-bit he studied Sanskrit and listened to many Dharma Masters lecture the Buddhadharma. Some people say this took him fourteen years. Others say it took nineteen. In general, he went through a great deal of suffering and difficulty to study the Buddhadharma and then when he had completed his studies, he returned to China.

When his return was imminent, the needles on the pine tree turned to the east. As soon as the Emperor saw that the pine needles were indeed pointing east, he knew that Dharma Master Hsuan Tsang was coming back and he sent out a party of officials to the western gate to welcome and escort him back. When they reached the gate, there indeed, was Dharma Master Hsuan Tsang returning.

Dharma Master Hsuan Tsang then concentrated on translating the Sutras and other works that he had brought back with him. He translated from Sanskrit into Chinese. At the time when he was translating the Great Prajna Sutra, within that one single year the peach trees blossomed six times. That was a sign of the auspiciousness of the Great Prajna Sutra and its importance to all of us. The fact that it was being translated moved even the wood and plants to display their delight.

Dharma Master Hsuan Tsang translated a great many Sutras. While in India, he bowed to the Buddha's Sharira and bones. He saw where the Buddha in a previous life had given up his eyes, and went to the place where the Buddha in a previous life had given up his head. He visited the place where the Buddha in a previous life had given up his life for the sake of a tiger. He also went to see the Bodhi tree under which the Buddha accomplished the Way. He went to all of those places celebrated in Buddhism. These pilgrimages are another indication of the extent of his true sincerity. While in India, whenever he met Dharma Masters, he never looked down on them, no matter how little they may have cultivated. He was extremely respectful. He was not the least bit arrogant or haughty. When he finished his studies, many Small Vehicle Dharma Masters and masters of externalist ways came to debate with him, but none were able to defeat him.

Dharma Master Hsuan Tsang is known as a TRIPITA[KA]
MASTER (Tripitaka = "Three Stores, Three Baskets").
The Tripitaka includes the Sutra Store, the Shastra
Store and the Vinaya Store. He was honored with thi[s]
title because he understood all three Stores without
any obstruction.

A Dharma Master is:

1. One who bestows the Dharma upon
   people.
2. One who takes the Dharma as his
   Master.

As to his name, HSUAN means "esoteric and
wonderful". He was esoteric in the sense that none
could really understand him. TSANG means "awe-
inspiring". He was awe-inspiring in that he could
do what others could not do. He was an outstanding
person among his peers. His wisdom surpassed all
those around him.

THE THREE CART PATRIARCH

At that time, Dharma Master Hsuan Tsang had eight hundred Bhikshus helping him translate the Sutras spoken by the Buddha. They were a group of extremely talented people. The most renowned among them was Dharma Master K'uei Chi. He was known as the "Three Cart Patriarch". Why was he called that? It's because prior to his leaving the home-life he presented some conditions to the Emperor. His consenting to the imperial edict he had received ordering him to leave the home-life was contingent upon being given three carts. He wanted these three carts to follow him wherever he went. One of these carts was to be filled with wine. Another cart was to carry fresh, juicy meat because he liked to eat it, and the third cart had to contain beautiful women. Now you see how he got his nickname. But you should be clear that the Three Cart Patriarch was not an ordinary person. For one thing, no ordinary person would dare present such conditions to the Emperor when he had been ordered to leave the home-life. In order to understand how special he was, we have to look into his previous life.

When Dharma Master Hsuan Tsang was on his way to India, he encountered an old cultivator way up in the mountains. The old cultivator had been meditating there for so long that the dust which had accumulated on his clothing was an inch or more thick. The birds had obviously made a seasonal thing of nesting in his hair. They built their nest, laid their eggs, and reared their young while he remained there in samadhi. It would be hard to say how many years he had been sitting in that same spot unmoving. Anyway, Dharma Master Hsuan Tsang rang his bell to bring him out of samadhi. The old fellow came out of samadhi all right, but he could not move. He was as stiff as a board. But he was able to ask, "Why did you ring the bell and bring me out of meditation?"

Dharma Master Hsuan Tsang asked him, "Old cultivator, how long have you been sitting here in samadhi? What is the sense of never coming out of meditation?"

The old cultivator replied, "I am waiting for the Red Yang Buddha to come into the world. Then I am going to help him propagate the Buddhadharma."

Dharma Master Hsuan Tsang said, "But the Red Yang Buddha has come and gone already. He entered the world and has already passed into Nirvana. You sat here and did not even know the Red Yang Buddhadharma was in the world."

"Well what time is it?" asked the cultivator, and Dharma Master Hsuan Tsang related that he was from the T'ang Dynasty. "That's all right," said the cultivator. "If the Red Yang Buddha has come and gone, I will wait for the White Yang Buddha," and he prepared to go back into samadhi.

Dharma Master Hsuan Tsang called him back, saying something like, "Old Bodhisattva!" or "Dhyana Companion!" or "Old Cultivator!" Those were the standard forms of address at that time. He said, "Do not go back into samadhi! It would be better if you followed me to help propagate the Buddhadharma. Although Shakyamuni Buddha, the Red Yang Buddha, has already gone to Nirvana, his Dharma is still in the world. Come along and help me spread the teaching."

"How can I help propagate it?" asked the old cultivator.

The Dharma Master said, "You go to Ch'ang An and when you come to the house with the yellow-tiled roof, get reborn there and you can eventually help propagatethe Dharma." He said this because the old cultivator's physical body was useless. He would have to trade it in on a new one. "You first go there and get reborn and when I get back you can help me propagate the Buddhadharma."

The old cultivator thought it over and agreed. So the old cultivator went off to rebirth in Ch'ang An and Dharma Master Hsuan Tsang went on his way to India to bring back the Sutras. When he got back, the first thing he did was congratulate the Emperor on the birth of his son. "I sent you back someone to be your son. That has been a happy event indeed!"

But the Emperor said, "No. I did not have a son while you were away."

"No?" said the Dharma Master, and so he looked into it and realized that the old cultivator had gotten off the track and been reborn in the house of the Defense Minister Yü Ch'ih Kung instead. Yü Ch'ih Kung was tough and had a black face. He was very talented and worked hard at his job, helping the Emperor maintain the country and rule the empire. Probably the old cultivator was a bit sloppy when he did things, so although Dharma Master Hsuan Tsang had told him clearly to get born in the house with the yellow-tiled roof, the old fellow got it wrong, chose the one with the blue tiles, and ended up becoming the nephew of the flamboyant Defense Minister. Perhaps you can imagine what it was like being the nephew of Yü Ch'ih Kung. As soon as he was old enough, he took a tremendous fancy to eating meat, drinking wine, and entertaining women. Perhaps, because he had cultivated for kalpas, sitting in samadhi without ever coming out, he had a few false thoughts like, "Meat is not bad as I recall. And I remember it was pleasant to drink wine. As for women, they were not bad either." So when he took rebirth, he could not put down the contents of those three carts.

But as soon as Dharma Master Hsuan Tsang learned from the Emperor that there was no prince, he checked things out and knew that the old cultivator was in fact Yü Ch'ih Kung's nephew. So he approached the Defense Minister and said, "You know, there is someone in your family whom I sent here to help propagate the Buddhadharma."

The Defense Minister said shortly, "Well, you told him to come, so you tell him to go." So he was told, but he would not go.

Finally Dharma Master Hsuan Tsang related the causes and conditions to Emperor T'ai Tsung who said immediately, "I will issue an Imperial Command and order him to leave home."

"Fine," said Master Hsuan Tsang. "But it is likely he will want to make it conditional. Whatever conditions he demands, just agree to them."

The Emperor agreed and thereupon commanded the nephew of Yü Ch'ih Kung to appear in court for an audience. "You must leave home," was the Emperor's order.

"If I want to leave home I will, and if I do not want to leave home, I won't."

"This is a royal command and if you do not obey it, you will be beheaded."

That put a scare into the nephew and so he complied, but he still had the nerve to set up three conditions. "I want a cart of meat, a cart of wine, and a cart of women to follow me wherever I go."

"Agreed," said the Emperor. So it was decided, The   nephew headed for Ta Hsing Shan -- "Great Flourishing Goodness" -- Monastery to leave the homelife. Since he was the son of an official, there was quite a fanfare.   As the procession neared the temple gates, the big bell was rung and the gigantic drum was beaten to welcome him. As soon as he heard the bell and drum he opened enlighten- ment and said, "Oh, that is the way it is. Originally, I was an old cultivator on that mountain." With a flick of his hand, he waved away the carts, "Take them back. I do not want them anymore." Although he dismissed the carts upon leaving home, people still called him the "Three Cart Patriarch."

KAO FENG MIAO OVERCOMES THE SLEEP DEMON

In Hangchow, China, there is a mountain peak called Inverted Lotus Flower located in Western Heavenly Eye, a division of the Five Heavenly Eyes mountain range. These Five Heavenly Eyes are called Eastern Heavenly Eye, Western Heavenly Eye, Northern Heavenly Eye, Southern Heavenly Eye, and Middle Heavenly Eye. They are called Heavenly Eyes because on the mountain peaks are pairs of springs which are like two eyes. Many people cultivate the Way there.

One of those who cultivated there was Ch'an Master Kao Feng Miao. Every time he sat down to meditate, he would fall asleep. He was obstructed in his cultivation by a kind of heavy torpor. Torpor is one of the twenty-six afflictions. It is a kind of dazed, thick-headed, unclear state of mind. When you meditate, you cannot enter samadhi if you are beset by torpor, and if you cannot enter samadhi, your mind becomes scattered. Being scattered is not gathering in your mind to one point.

Why did Ch'an Master Kao Feng Miao go to the Heavenly Eye Mountains to cultivate? He wanted to find a way to cure himself of torpor. He knew that if he fell asleep while meditating on Inverted Lotus Flower Peak, he would fall off a cliff thousands of feet high and splatter on the ground below. He decided to put his life on the line and go to that peak to cultivate the Way, sitting on the edge of that ten-thousand foot cliff. If he fell asleep there, it would be the end.

He meditated for one day and did not sleep. Then for another day he did not sleep. Three days went by, and still no sleep. But on the fourth day, he finally dozed off. As soon as he fell asleep, he rocked forward and lurched off the cliff. He had fallen about nine thousand feet when he finally woke up, but suddenly, before he hit the ground, a hand appeared to catch him.

After this miraculous rescue, he asked, "Who has saved me?"

His rescuer answered, "Dharma Protector Wei T'ou."

When he heard that the Dharma Protector Wei T'ou Bodhisattva had saved him, he was very happy, and he began having arrogant thoughts. "I must be very special." He asked, "Elder Wei, how many people in the world can cultivate like me?"

The Bodhisattva Wei T'ou replied, "Cultivators like you are as numerous as the hairs on an ox. You are really shameless. I will not protect your dharma for eighty thousand great kalpas." When the Bodhisattva left, Kao Feng Miao cried and cried. He was really sorry for being so stuck up. He thought, "This is terrible! I am certainly not a cultivator of the Way. When the Bodhisattva Wei T'ou came to protect my dharma, how could I have had such arrogant thoughts?"

His shame and remorse kept him in tears for a long time and then suddenly he thought, "Hey! Before, when I cultivated the Way at the edge of the cliff, I did not know that the Bodhisattva Wei T'ou was protecting my dharma, but I cultivated there nonetheless. I did not think that I could only cultivate the Way by relying on Wei T'ou

Bodhisattva. Now that he is not protecting my dharma, should I quit? Certainly not! I should still cultivate the Way!"

He decided to go back up the mountain to meditate. This time he was even more vigorous and vowed, "Even if I die, I will cultivate the Way. I will meditate. My life is not important unless I can accomplish my karma in the Way."

So he tried it again. He climbed back up the mountain and started meditating again. This time, he worked even harder at staying awake. He sat meditating for one, two, three days without dozing off, but then started to get sleepy again. Even though he was trying not to, he still fell asleep, and rolled off the cliff. When he had fallen about halfway, someone saved him again. After he was rescued, he asked, "Who is protecting my dharma?"

His protector answer, "Wei T'ou."

Ch'an Master Kao Feng Miao got angry. "Elder Wei, so you lie too, huh? You said you would not protect my dharma for eighty thousand great kalpas, but you have saved me again. Haven't you told a lie?"

The Bodhisattva Wei T'ou said, "No, I have not lied. I will explain it to you. Because of your arrogance, I said I would not protect your dharma, but afterwards, you repented and reformed, eighty thousand great kalpas' worth. So again, I protected your dharma."

This story tells how kalpas can be but one thought. In one thought, the Ch'an Master Kao Feng Miao went beyond eighty thousand great kalpas. He really meant it when he said he was sorry. So it erased the mistake he made before.

MAHAKASHYAPA

MAHA means great, many, and victorious.
The Sanskrit word KASHYAPA means "great turtle
clan", because Mahakashyapa's ancestors saw the
map on the back of a giant turtle and used it to
cultivate the Way.

Kashyapa also means "light-drinking clan,"
because his body shone with a light which was so
bright it seemed to "drink up" all other light.

Why did his body shine? Seven Buddhas ago,
in the time of the Buddha Vipasyin, there was a
poor woman who decided to repair a ruined temple.
The roof of the temple had been blown off and the
images inside were exposed to the wind and rain.
The woman went everywhere and asked for help, and
when she had collected enough money she asked a
goldsmith to put new gold on the images. By the
time he was finished, the goldsmith fell in love
with her and said, "You have attained great merit
from this work, but we should share it. You may
supply the gold and I will furnish the labor,
free." So the temple was rebuilt and the images
regilded. The goldsmith asked the woman to marry
him and, in every life, for ninety-one kalpas,
they were husband and wife and their bodies shone
with purple and golden light.

Mahakashyapa was born in India, in Magadha.
When he was twenty his father and mother wanted
him to marry, but he said, "The woman I marry
must shine with golden light. Unless you find
such a woman, I won't marry." Eventually, they
found one, and they were married. As a result of

their good karma, their bodies shone with gold light and they cultivated together and investigated the doctrines of the Way. When Mahakashyapa left home to become a Bhiksu, his wife became a Bhiksuni called "Purple and Golden Light."

Mahakashyapa's personal name was "Pippala", because his parents prayed to the spirit of a pippala tree to grant them a son.

As the First Patriarch, Mahakashyapa holds an important position in Buddhism. When Shakyamuni Buddha spoke the Dharma, the Great Brahma Heaven King presented him with a golden lotus and Shakyamuni Buddha held up the flower before the assembly. At that time, hundreds of thousands of gods and men were present, but no one responded except Mahakashyapa, who simply smiled. Then the Buddha said, "I have the Right Dharma-Eye Treasury, the wonderful mind of Nirvana, the real mark which is unmarked. This Dharma-door of mind-to-mind transmission has been transmitted to Kashyapa." Thus, Mahakashyapa received the transmission of Dharma and became the first Buddhist Patriarch.

Venerable Mahakashyapa is still present in the world. When he left home under the Buddha, he was already one hundred and sixty years old. By the time Shakyamuni Buddha had spoken Dharma for forty-nine years in over three hundred Dharma assemblies, Kashyapa was already over two hundred years old. After Shakyamuni Buddha entered Nirvana, Kasyapa went to Southwestern China to Chicken Foot Mountain in Yunnan Province. It has been over three thousand years since the Buddha's Nirvana, but Mahakashyapa is still sitting in samadhi in Chicken Foot Mountain waiting for

Maitreya Buddha to appear in the world. At that
time, he will give Maitreya the bowl which the
Four Heavenly Kings gave Shakyamuni Buddha and
which Shakyamuni Buddha gave him, and his work in
this world will be finished.

Many cultivators travel to Chicken Foot
Mountain to worship the Patriarch Kashyapa, and
on the mountain, there are always three kinds of
light: Buddha light, gold light, and silver light.
Those with sincere hearts can hear a big bell
ringing inside the mountain. It rings by itself,
and although you cannot see it, you can hear it
for several hundred miles. It is an inconceivable
state.

VAKKULA

VAKKULA means "good bearing". He was extremely handsome. In the past, during the time of Vipasyin Buddha, he made offerings of the Indian haritaki fruit to a Pratyeka Buddha, a sage enlightened to conditions. Because of this, he received the retribution of long life in every life for ninety-one aeons. Foremost of the disciples in age, he lived to be a hundred and sixty.

In past lives, Vakkula kept the precept against killing so well that he never killed a single creature, not even grass or trees. Thus, he obtained "five kinds of death-free retribution."

Vakkula was a strange child. He was not born crying like most children, but entered the world smiling. Not only was he smiling, he was sitting upright in full lotus. Seeing this, his mother exclaimed, "He's a monster!" and threw him in the fire place. After three or four hours, he had not burned; he just sat there in full lotus laughing. Fully convinced that he was a monster, she then tried to boil him. When she took the cover off the pot several hours later, he just smiled back at her. "Oh no!" she cried, and threw him into the ocean. He did not drown, however, because a big fish swam up and swallowed him whole. Than a man caught the fish in a net. When the fisherman cut open the fish, Vakkula was not cut by the knife. He stepped right out of the fish. He was not hurt at all. The fire did not burn him, the water did not boil him, the ocean did not drown him, the fish did not chomp him to death, and the fisherman's knife did not cut him. Because he kept the precept

against killing in every life, he obtained these
"five kinds of death-free retribution."

PINDOLA BHARADVAJA

Pindola Bharadvaja was a disciple of Shakyamuni Buddha. His name means "unmoving sharp roots."
Pindola Bharadvaja still lives in the world,which
makes him over three thousand years old. He has
not entered Nirvana because he broke a rule.

Once an elder called Jyotiska carved a bowl
out of sandalwood, put it on top of a high pole,
and said, "Whoever can use his spiritual powers to
get the bowl can have it." Many of those who be-
longed to externalist ways tried, but none succeed-
ed. One day, Pindola and Mahamaudgalyayana were
sitting together on a huge boulder. Pindola told
Mahamaudgalyayana about the sandalwood bowl and
suggested he get it, but Mahamaudgalyayana replied,
"I don't want to display my spiritual powers before the laypeople. You can get the bowl if you
want."

Thereupon Pindola soared into the sky, and,
still sitting atop that huge boulder, encircled
the City of Shravasti three times. This alarmed
the citizens so much that they ran about in dismay,
fearing that the huge rock was going to fall down
and crush them. Pindola then flew up to the top
of the pole and took the sandalwood bowl with ease.

On seeing this feat, the Elder Jyotiska put
his palms together respectfully and said to Pindola, "Please wait, Venerable One!" He then took
the bowl and filled it with delicious food and
offered it to Pindola. All the people knew who

got the sandalwood bowl. The Buddha knew too, but he rebuked Pindola, "How could you have made a display of your spiritual powers just for the sake of a worthless bowl? Because you have acted badly, you can no longer stay in Jambudvipa. Go to Aparagodaniya, the Western Continent, and propagate the Dharma there." So Pindola went to the Western Continent.

After a while, the people of Jambudvipa started to miss Pindola and wondered when he would return. Because of that, the Buddha allowed him to come back to Jambudvipa. One time, after Pindola's return, the daughter of the Benefactor of the Orphans and the Solitary wnated to make offerings to the Buddha and the Sangha. She invited them all. Some of the Bhikshus who had spiritual powers went by air. Pindola was then staying on a mountain, and he went by air too, bringing that mountain along with him. When the Buddha saw the sight he was displeased and again scolded Pindola, "There you go again, showing off your spiritual powers! Because you have broken that rule again, I now forbid you to enter Nirvana. You must stay in the world forever to act as a field of blessings for living beings. Protect and uphold my Dharma so that it will never become extinct!"

A hundred years after the Buddha entered Nirvana, the great King Ashoka was reigning over India. One day he prepared all kinds of food and provisions to make offerings to the Sangha. He was careful to do everything right in order to properly show his respect. First, he himself received the Eight Lay Precepts. Then he put on clean clothing and adorned his palace with various kinds of jeweled canopies, banners, flowers, and incense. He sincerely bowed to the four directions, and made the following request, "All the worthy disciples of the Buddha, please have compassion and come here to receive my humble offerings."

In response to the King's sincere request, three hundred thousand of the Buddha's disciples came. One hundred thousand of them were Arhats of the fourth fruition, while the rest were first, second, and third fruition Arhats, and commoners as well. But nobody took the foremost seat. King Ashoka wondered why not. The answer was, "The first seat belongs to the Venerable Pindola Bharadvaja. The Buddha personally assigned him to this position. Who else would dare take the first seat, since the Venerable One is the most senior member among us Bhikshus in the world!"

At that time, Pindola, together with an uncountable number of Arhats came flying through the air. He was magnificent, like a King of Swans. Everybody stood up and paid their respects. King Ashoka was overjoyed at seeing the Venerable One, who assumed the appearance of a Pratyekabuddha. His hair was as white as snow and his eyebrows were long enough to cover his two eyes. After bowing to the Venerable One, King Ashoka asked him, "So the Venerable One has personally seen the Buddha?"

Pindola lifted his long eyebrows away from his eyes with one hand so he could see the King, and replied, "Yes, I personally drew near to the Buddha. In fact, Great King, in your previous life, you also made an offering to the Buddha. One day, in your former life, when you were a little boy, the Buddha and his retinue happened to pass down the street where you were playing. You, as that boy, made a small offering of sand to the Buddha. The Buddha then predicted that you would someday become a great King named Ashoka who would build 84,000 stupas to store his sharira. I, too, was present in the assembly at that time."

The King asked, "Where does the Venerable One live now?"

Pindola answered, "I live on a mountain in the north, called Gandhamara, with sixty thousand Arhats."

A thousand years later in China, during the T'ang dynasty, the Venerable Pindola appeared in a dream to Vinaya Master Tao Hsüan to praise him for his efforts in propagating the Vinaya. Within Buddhism there are ceremonies for inviting the Venerable Pindola Bharadvaja. Some people have been extremely sincere in performing these ceremonies to make their request, and the Venerable Pindola has appeared in their midst assuming the appearance of an ordinary bhikshu. He never looks strange or out of place. But as proof of his presence, the flowers which are offered to him will not wither.

GAVAMPATI

This Venerable One's strange name means "cow cud." Far in the distant past, he had insulted a Bhikshu who could not eat hard things and had to slurp his food because his teeth were no good. "You eat like a cow!" said Gavampati. The old Bhikshu happened to be a Pratyeka Buddha, and because of Gavampati's careless slander, Gavampati was reborn for five hundred lifetimes as a cow and got to know the real bitterness that it involved.

Finally, he met Shakyamuni Buddha, learned to cultivate, and attained Arhatship. Although he had certified to the fruit, his habits from so many lives remained unchanged, and all day he snorted like a cow chewing its cud. Shakyamuni Buddha was afraid that someone might slander him and reap the same reward, and so he sent the Venerable Gavampati to heaven to live. There he became the foremost of those who receive the offerings of the gods.

We should take care not to speak rashly or to scold others. If you make fun of others, others will make fun of you.

THE HORSE WHO HEARD THE <u>DHARMA FLOWER SUTRA</u>

Once there was a Bhikshu in China who served
as an advisor to the Emperor. Every day, when he
left the monastery to go to the Court, as soon as he
mounted his horse, he began reciting The <u>Dharma
Flower Sutra</u> from memory. By the time he arrived
at the Palace, he had recited the first roll.
Suddenly one day his horse died. At the same
moment, a son was born in the house of a layman
who lived across from the monastery. When the
child was born, his mother had an inconceivable
dream. She dreamt the monk's horse came galloping
up to her house and ran right into her chest. Just
then she gave birth to the child. Thinking her
dream very unusual, she told her relatives to go
see if the horse was at the monastery. Sure
enough, they discovered that the horse had just
died. She knew, then, that the horse had been
reborn as her son and so she sent him to the
monastery right away to become a monk.

The child was really stupid. No matter how
the monks tried, there was no way to teach him to
read or write. He could not read a single word
and simply could not be taught. One day, a
Bhikshu began to teach him The <u>Dharma Flower Sutra</u>,
saying it out loud, word by word and he learned it
right away. He learned the entire first roll in
no time, but could not remember any of the second
roll at all. Why was this? When he was a horse,
he had heard the monk recite the first roll every
day on his way to the Court and so he could
remember it. Because the horse had heard the Sutra
recited every day, it got reborn as a person. It

135

is clear that the merit and virtue of The <u>Dharma Flower Sutra</u> is inconceivable.

ICE LOTUS BHIKSHU

There was once a monk who recited The _Dharma Flower Sutra_ every day. In a single day you can just barely get through the entire seven rolls of the Sutra. The Sutra says that the merit and virtue obtained by one who copies the Sutra out is inconceivable. So, the monk decided to write it out. Stroke by stroke, word by word, he reverently copied it without making a single mistake. He finished in the middle of a cold Manchurian winter. When he put his brush in the water to rinse it out, the water froze to form a lotus on the brush-tip and continued to freeze forming a larger and larger lotus. Because of this, he gave himself the name "The Ice-lotus Bhikshu." The lotus appeared in response to his utmost sincerity.

Many people saw this event. It really happened! Wouldn't you say it was a wonderful dharma?

GREAT BODHISATTVAS

What is Bodhisattva? Bodhisattva is a Sanskrit word. Bodhi means "enlightenment " and sattva means "being." The word means "to enlighten those with sentience," that is, to cause living beings to wake up.

Bodhisattva also means "enlightened among beings" because Bodhisattvas themselves are awake. Enlightenment is simply the opposite of confusion; confusion is simply non-enlightenment. With one enlightened thought, you are a Buddha. With one confused thought you are a living being. With every thought enlightened in every thought you are a Buddha. With every thought confused, in every thought you are a living being.

Bodhisattvas are beings who can wake themselves up. Every day they are more enlightened, not more confused.

Bodhisattvas are enlightened beings and living beings are confused beings. Enlightened beings are those who are enlightened among all the confused living beings. In all situations, they are awake. And so it is said,

If you recognize things for what they are
You can leap over the common world.
Confused by what you see,
You fall beneath the turning wheel.

Bodhisattvas transcend the world; living beings fall beneath the grinding wheel of birth and death. The difference between Bodhisattvas and living beings is the difference between enlightenment and confusion. We say, "Enlightened, you're a Buddha." Enlightened, too, you are a Bodhisattva. Confused, you're a being

THE BUDDHIST TEXT TRANSLATION SOCIETY

CHAIRPERSON: The Venerable Tripitaka Master Hsüan Hua
-Abbot of Gold Mountain Monastery, Gold
Wheel Monastery, and Tathagata Monastery
-Chancellor of Dharma Realm Buddhist
University
-Professor of the Tripitaka and the Dhyanas

PRIMARY TRANSLATION COMMITTEE:

Chairpersons: Venerable Tripitaka Master Hsüan Hua
Bhikshuni Heng Ch'ih

Members:

Bhikshu Heng Sure
Bhikshu Heng Kuan
Bhikshu Heng Shun
Bhikshu Heng Ch'au
Bhikshu Heng Tso
Bhikshu Heng Ch'i
Bhikshu Heng Gung
Bhikshu Heng Wu
Bhikshu Heng Jau
Bhikshu Heng Ch'ang

Bhikshuni Heng Ch'ing
Bhikshuni Heng Chü
Bhikshuni Heng Chai
Bhikshuni Heng Wen

Bhikshuni Heng Tao
Bhikshuni Heng Ming
Bhikshuni Heng Hsien

Bhikshuni Heng Tsai
Bhikshuni Heng Duan
Bhikshuni Heng Bin
Bhikshuni Heng Liang
Bhikshuni Heng Lyan
Bhikshuni Heng Chia
Upasika Terri Nicholson
Upasaka David Rounds
Upasaka R.B. Epstein
Upasaka Chou Li-jen

REVIEWING COMMITTEE:

Chairpersons: Bhikshu Heng Tso
Upasaka Kuo Jung Epstein

Members:

Bhikshu Heng Sure
Bhikshu Heng Kuan
Bhikshu Heng Gung
Bhikshu Heng Wu
Bhikshuni Heng Ch'ih
Bhikshuni Heng Chai
Bhikshuni Heng Wen
Bhikshuni Heng Tao

Bhikshuni Heng Hsien
Bhikshuni Heng Tsai
Bhikshuni Heng Duan
Bhikshuni Heng Bin
Bhikshuni Heng Liang
Upasika Hsieh Ping-ying
Upasaka David Rounds
Upasaka Chou Li-jen

EDITING COMMITTEE:

Chairperson: Upasika Susan Rounds

Advisor: Bhikshu Heng Kuan

Members:

Bhikshu Heng Sure
Bhikshu Heng Lai
Bhikshu Heng Shun
Bhikshu Heng Ch'au
Bhikshu Heng Tso
Bhikshu Heng Ch'i
Bhikshu Heng Wu
Bhikshu Heng Jau
Bhikshuni Heng Ch'ih
Bhikshuni Heng Ch'ing
Bhikshuni Heng Chü
Bhikshuni Heng Chai
Bhikshuni Heng Wen
Bhikshuni Heng Tao
Bhikshuni Heng Ming
Bhikshuni Heng Hsien

Bhikshuni Heng Tsai
Bhikshuni Heng Duan
Bhikshuni Heng Bin
Bhikshuni Heng Liang
Bhikshuni Heng Lyan
Bhikshuni Heng Chia
Upasaka R.B. Epstein
Upasaka David Rounds
Upasika Nancy Lethcoe
Upasika Terri Nicholson
Upasaka Chou Li-jen
Upasika Phuong Kuo Wu
Upasika Janice V. Storss
Upasaka Douglas Powers
Upasika Marion Robertson
Upasika Marla Wong

CERTIFYING COMMITTEE:

Chairperson: Venerable Tripitaka Master Hsüan Hua

Members:

Bhikshu Heng Sure
Bhikshu Heng Kuan
Bhikshu Heng Tso
Bhikshuni Heng Ch'ih
Bhikshuni Heng Ch'ing
Bhikshuni Heng Wen

Bhikshuni Heng Tao
Bhikshuni Heng Hsien
Upasaka Wong Kuo Chün
Upasika Terri Nicholson
Upasaka R.B. Epstein
Upasika Janice V. Storss

CHINESE PUBLICATIONS COMMITTEE:

Chairperson: Upasaka Chou Li-jen

Members:

Bhikshuni Heng Lyan
Upasika Phuong Kuo Wu
Upasika Yao-sen Epstein

Bina Teng
Wong Kuo Ch'ang

Dharma Protector Wei To Bodhisattva

Verse of Transference

May the merit and virtue accrued from this work,
Adorn the Buddhas' Pure Lands,
Repaying four kinds of kindness above,
And aiding those suffering in the paths below.

May those who see and hear of this,
All bring forth the resolve for Bodhi,
And when this retribution body is over,
Be born together in ultimate bliss.

All of the translation works by the Buddhist Text Translation Society are accompanied by interlinear commentaries by the Venerable Tripitaka Master Hsüan Hua, and are available in softcover only, unless otherwise noted.

BUDDHIST SUTRAS

Amitabha Sutra - This Sutra, which was spoken by the Buddha without being formally requested as in other Sutras, explains the causes and circumstances for rebirth in the Land of Ultimate Bliss of Amitabha (Limitless Light) Buddha. The commentary includes extensive information on common Buddhist terminology, and stories on many of the Buddha's foremost disciples. ISBN 0-917512-01-4, 204 pgs., $8.00 (Also available in Spanish. $8.00)

Brahma Net Sutra　梵網經講錄　The Buddha explains the Ten Major and Forty-eight Minor Precepts of the Bodhisattva. Bi-lingual edition, English-Zhung Wen.Vol. 1, ISBN 0-917512-79-0, 300 pgs. Vol. 2, ISBN 0-917512-88-X, 210 pgs. Two volume set is $18.00. The commentary to this work is by the late Venerable Master Hui Seng.

Dharani Sutra - This Sutra tells of the past causes and conditions of the Bodhisattva of Great Compassion, Avalokiteshvara (Kuan Yin), and the various ways of practicing the Great Compassion Mantra. It is a fundamental Secret School text. The second half of the publication is divided up into three sections. The first explains the meaning of the mantra line by line. The second has Zhung Wen poems and drawings of division bodies of Kuan Yin Bodhisattva for each of the 84 lines of the mantra. The last section contains drawings and verses in English on each of the 42 Hands and Eyes of Kuan Yin. This is the first English translation of this scripture. ISBN 0-917512-13-8, 352 pgs., $12.00

大悲心陀羅尼經　has all of the material noted above for the DHARANI SUTRA, except the commentary and the section explaining the meaning of the mantra. All the material is in Zhung Wen only.210 pgs., $6.00.

Dharma Flower (Lotus) Sutra - In this Sutra, which was spoken in the last period of the Buddha's teaching, the Buddha proclaims the ultimate principles of the Dharma which unites all previous teachings into one. When completed, the entire Sutra will be from 15 to 20 volumes. The following are those volumes which have been published to date:

Volume I, Introductory section. Discusses the five periods and eight teachings of the T'ien T'ai School and then analyzes the School's Five Profound Meanings as they relate to the Sutra. The last portion tells of the life of Tripitaka Master Kumarajiva, who translated the Sutra from Sanskrit to Zhung Wen. ISBN 0-917512-16-2, 85 pgs., $3.95

Volume II, Introduction, Chapter One. Describes the setting for the Sutra, which includes the assembly that gathered to hear it, the Buddha's emission of light, the questioning of Maitreya Bodhisattva, and the response given by Manjushri Bodhisattva. ISBN 0-917512-22-1, 324 pgs., $7.95

Volume III, Expedient Methods, Chapter Two. After the Buddha emerges from samadhi he speaks of the vast merit and virtue of the Buddhas. Shariputra beseeches him to expound further on this. After his third request, the Buddha consents, and for the first time proclaims that all beings without exception can become Buddhas. ISBN 0-917512-26-X, 183 pgs., $7.95

Volume IV, A Parable, Chapter Three. The Buddha explains the purpose of his teachings by means of an analogy of an Elder who tries to rescue five hundred children who are absorbed in play in a burning house. ISBN 0-917-512-62-6, 371 pgs., $8.95

Volume V, Belief and Understanding, Chapter Four. Four of the Buddha's foremost Arhat disciples relate a parable about a prodigal son to express their joy that they too, will become Buddhas. ISBN 0-917512-64-2, 200 pgs., $6.95

Volume VI, Medicinal Herbs, Chapter Five, & Conferring Predictions, Chapter Six. The Buddha uses the analogy of a rain-cloud to illustrate how his teaching benefits all beings. ISBN 0-917-512-65-0, 161 pgs., $6.95

Volume VII, Parable of the Transformation City, Chapter Seven. The Buddha teaches that the attainment of his Arhat disciples is like a city which he conjured up as an expedient when they became weary of the journey to Buddhahood. ISBN 0-917-512-93-6, 250 pgs., $7.95

Volume VIII, Five Hundred Disciples Receive Predictions, Chapter Eight, & Bestowing Predictions Upon Those Studying and Beyond Study, Chapter Nine. More than a thousand disciples receive predictions that they will become Buddhas in the future. ISBN 0-917-512-71-5, 160 pgs., $6.95

Volume IX, Masters of the Dharma, Chapter Ten & Vision of the Jewelled Stupa, Chapter Eleven. Chapter Ten explains the vast merit from upholding and propagating the LOTUS SUTRA, and in Chapter Eleven, all the transformation bodies of Shakyamuni Buddha gather so that those in the assembly can see Many Jewels Buddha. ISBN 0-917-512-85-5, 270 pgs., $9.00

Volume X, Devadatta, Chapter Twelve & Exhortation to Maintain, Chapter Thirteen. In Chapter Twelve, the Buddha reveals that Devadatta was once his teacher in a former life and then bestows a prediction of Buddhahood on him. The eight year old dragon girl becomes a Buddha. In Chapter Thirteen, the Buddha bestows predictions of Buddhahood on Bhikshunis. ISBN 0-88139-34-0, 150 pgs., $5.00

Volume XI, Peaceful & Happy Conduct, Chapter Fourteen. Elucidates the "places of closeness" that a Bodhisattva should draw near to and places he should stay apart from. Discusses the body, mouth, and mind karma of cultivators and the importance of vows. ISBN 0-88139-022-4.

Universal Door Chapter. Zhung Wen. $5.00
妙法蓮華經觀世音菩薩普門品淺釋

Further Volumes Forthcoming

Flower Adornment (Avatamsaka) Sutra 大方廣佛華嚴經淺釋
Known as the 'King of Kings' of all Buddhist scriptures because of its profundity and great length (81 rolls containing more than 700,000 Zhung Wen characters).It contains the most complete explanation of the Buddha's state and the Bodhisattva's quest for Awakening. When completed, the entire Sutra-text with commentary is estimated to be from 75 to 100 volumes. The following are those volumes which have been published to date:

Verse Preface 華嚴經疏序淺釋 *a succinct and eloquent verse commentary by T'ang Dynasty National Master Ch'ing Liang who was the Master of seven emperors. The Preface gives a complete explanation of all the fundamental principles contained in the Sutra. This is the first English translation of this text. Bi-lingual edition, English & Zhung Wen.ISBN 0-917512-28-6, 244 pgs., $7.00*

Prologue - *a detailed explanation of the principles of the Sutra by National Master Ch'ing Liang, utilizing the Hsien Shou method of analyzing scriptures known as the Ten Doors. The PROLOGUE contains the first Nine Doors. Will be approximately 7 to 10 volumes upon completion. The following volumes have been published to date:*

First Door, *The Causes and Conditions for the Arisal of the Teaching of the FLOWER ADORNMENT SUTRA. Complete in one volume. ISBN 0-917512-66-9, 252 pgs., $10.00*
Second Door, *The Stores and Teachings in Which It (THE FLOWER ADORNMENT SUTRA) is contained, in three volumes:*

Part One, *Complete discussion of Three Stores; beginning of discussion of the Schools in Zhung Kuo. ISBN 0-917512-73-1, 280 pgs., $10.00*
Part Two, *More on Zhung Wen Schools. The Indian Schools, and comparisons among them. ISBN 0-917512-98-7, 220 pgs., $10.00*
Part Three, *Detailed discussion of the Five Hsien Shou Teachings. The sequence of the Teaching Methods, and the inconceivable state of the Flower Adornment. ISBN 0-88139-009-7, 160 pgs., $8.00*

Further Volumes Forthcoming

華嚴經疏淺釋 *the entire text and commentary of the Ten Doors in Zhung Wen.Four volume set, $27.00*

Flower Store Adorned Sea of Worlds, Chapter 5, Part 1. *Describes the universe we live in, including an explanation of principles pertaining to the coming into being of worlds, the wind wheels that uphold them, their orbits, mutual attraction, and detailed descriptions of the worlds located on the 20 tiers of the lotus that forms the basis of our cosmic structure. ISBN 0-917512-54-5, 250 pgs. $8.50*

The Names of the Thus Come Ones, *Chapter 7. In this chapter,
the Bodhisattvas gather from the worlds of the ten directions to
request the Buddha to speak about the Great Bodhisattva practices
which are explained at great length in later chapters of the FLOWER
ADORNMENT SUTRA.* This volume also includes *Chapter 8,* The Four
Holy Truths. *Each of the Four Holy Truths--Suffering, Accumulation,
Extinction, and the Way--are explained according to the conditions
of ten different worlds plus the Saha World, the world which we
inhabit.* ISBN 0-88139-014-3.

Bright Enlightenment, *Chapter 9. Shakyamuni Buddha emits light
from the soles of his feet which continually gets brighter and shines
upon more and different countries in the ten directions. After
each time that he emits light, Manjushri Bodhisattva speaks verses
praising the virtues of the Buddha.* ISBN 0-88139-005-4, 225 pgs.,
$8.50

Pure Conduct, *Chapter 11. This chapter of the Sutra gives a
detailed explanation of the pure practices of the Bodhisattva. It
is one of the most renowned guides to the Vinaya in the Buddhist
Canon.* ISBN 0-917512-37-5, 255 pgs., $9.00

Ten Dwellings, *Chapter 15. Explains the state of the Ten Dwellings attained by the Bodhisattva.* ISBN 0-917512-77-4, 185 pgs., $8.00

Brahma Conduct, *Chapter 16. Explains the meanings of the pure
Brahma conduct cultivated by the Bodhisattva.* ISBN 0-917512-80-4,
65 pgs., $4.00

The Merit and Virtue From First Bringing Forth The Mind, *Chapter
17. Uses various analogies to describe the merit obtained by the
Bodhisattva when he first resolves his mind on becoming Enlightened.*
ISBN 0-917512-83-9, 200 pgs., $7.00

The Ten Inexhaustible Treasuries, *Chapter 22. Explains the Ten
Inexhaustible Treasuries attained by the Bodhisattva, which immediately proceed the Ten Conducts.* ISBN 0-917512-38-3, 184 pgs.,
$7.00

Praises in the Tushita Heaven Palace, *Chapter 24. Verses in
praise of the Buddha spoken by the great Bodhisattvas after the
Buddha had arrived in the Tushita Heaven, prior to Vajra Banner
Bodhisattva's explanation of the Ten Transferences.* ISBN 0-917512-
39-1, 130 pgs., $5.00

Ten Transferences, *Chapter 25, Part 1. Detailed prose and verse
discussion of these important Bodhisattva stages. Contains the
First Transference of Saving and Protecting Living Beings Apart
From the Mark of Living Beings, and the Second Transference of In-
destructibility which discusses faith.* ISBN 0-917512-52-9, 250 pgs.,
$8.50

Ten Grounds, *Chapter 26, Part 1. Contains the First Ground of
Happiness, which focuses on the practice of giving.* ISBN 0-917512-
87-1, 234 pgs., $7.00. *Part 2. Covers the Bodhisattva's Second
Ground of Leaving Filth, Third Ground of Emitting Light, and the
Fourth Ground of Blazing Wisdom.* ISBN 0-917512-74-X, 200 pgs., $8.00

Further Volumes Forthcoming

十地品 The Ten Grounds with commentary, in Zhung Wen. Three volume set $17.00

Universal Worthy's Conduct, Chapter 36. Universal Worthy Bodhisattva explains obstructions that arise from anger, gives methods to correct it, and describes the purities, wisdoms, universal entrances and supremely wonderous minds that result. ISBN 0-88139-011-9, 78 pgs., $7.50

Entering the Dharma Realm, Chapter 39. This chapter, which makes up one quarter of the entire Sutra, contains the spiritual journey of the Youth Good Wealth in his search for Ultimate Awakening. In his quest he meets fifty-three 'Good Teachers,' each of whom represents a successive stage on the Bodhisattva Path. The following volumes have been published to date:

Part One. Describes the setting for the youth's quest, and his meeting with Manjushri Bodhisattva. ISBN 0-917512-68-5, 280 pgs., $8.50

Part Two. In this volume, Good Wealth meets his first ten teachers, who represent the positions of the Ten Dwellings. ISBN 0-917512-70-7, 250 pgs., $8.50

Part Three. In this volume, Good Wealth is taught by the ten teachers who correspond to the Ten Conducts. ISBN 0-917512-73-1, 250 pgs., $8.50

Part Four. In this volume, Good Wealth meets the ten teachers who represent the Bodhisattvas of the Ten Transferences. ISBN 0-917512-76-6, 185 pgs., $8.00

Part Five. In this volume, Good Wealth meets the six teachers who represent the first six Grounds. ISBN 0-917512-81-2, 300 pgs., $9.00

Part Six. Good Wealth meets the teachers on the seventh to tenth Grounds. ISBN 0-917512-48-0, 320 pgs., $9.00

Universal Worthy's Conduct and Vows, Chapter 40. A detailed explanation of Universal Worthy Bodhisattva's ten great kinds of practice, considered to be the foremost of all practices. ISBN 0-917512-84-7, 300 pgs., $10.00 (In Zhung Wen, $4.00)

華嚴經 - World Rulers' Adornments, Chapter 1 to the Ten Transferences (parts 1 to 3), Chapter 25. In Zhung Wen only. Includes commentary. Ten Volume set $60.00. Vol. 9 $8.00; Vol. 10 $8.00.

Heart Sutra and Verses Without a Stand - Considered the most popular Sutra in the world today, the text of the HEART SUTRA explains the meaning of Prajna-paramita: the perfection of wisdom, which is able to clearly perceive the emptiness of all phenomena. Each line in the text is accompanied by an eloquent verse by the Venerable Master Hua, and his commentary contains an explanation of most of the fundamental Buddhist concepts. ISBN 0-917512-28-7, 160 pgs., $7.50

心經非台頌解 Same as HEART SUTRA above, including the commentary. In Zhung Wen. 120 pgs., $5.00

Shurangama Sutra - This Sutra gives the most detailed explanation of the Buddha's teachings concerning the mind. It includes an analysis of where the mind is located, an explanation of the origin of the cosmos, the specific workings of karma, a description of all the realms of existence, and the fifty kinds of deviant samadhi-concentrations which can delude us in our search for awakening. Also, in this Sutra, twenty-five enlightened Sages explain the methods they used to become enlightened. The entire eight volume set is available at a discounted price of $65.00.

Volume One, The Venerable Ananda presents seven ideas on the location of the mind, and the Buddha shows how each one is incorrect, and then explains the roots of the false and the true. ISBN 0-917512-17-0, 289 pgs., $8.50

Volume Two, The Buddha explains individual and collective karma, and reveals the true mind by displaying ten different aspects of the seeing-nature. ISBN 0-917512-25-1, 212 pgs, $8.50

Volume Three, The Buddha gives a clear description of the qualities of all the sensefields, their respective consciousnesses, and all the internal and external elemental forces of the universe. He explains how all are ultimately unreal, neither existing through causes nor arising spontaneously. ISBN 0-917512-94-4, 240 pgs, $8.50

Volume Four, The Buddha talks about the formation of the world, the coming into being of sentient creatures, and the cycle of karmic retribution. ISBN 0-917512-90-1, 200 pgs, $8.50

Volume Five, Twenty-five Sages explain the method they used to transcend the realm of birth and death. Manjushri Bodhisattva selects the method used by the Bodhisattva Kuan Yin of 'returning the hearing to listen to the self-nature,' as the most appropriate for people in our world-system. ISBN 0-917512-91-X, 250 pgs., $8.50

Volume Six, Includes the Buddha's explanation of the Four Clear and Unalterable Instructions on Purity, how to establish a Bodhi-mandala, the Shurangama Mantra and its wondrous functions, and the 12 categories of living beings. ISBN 0-917512-97-9, 200 pgs., $8.50

Volume Seven, Contains an explanation of the 55 stages of the Bodhisattva's path to Enlightenment, how beings fall into the hells, all the realms of existence of the ghosts, animals, people, immortals, and the various heavens. ISBN 0-917512-97-9, 270 pgs., $8.50

Volume Eight, In this, the final volume, the Buddha explains the Fifty Skandha Demon States, which cultivators may get stuck in. ISBN 0-917512-35-9, $8.50 (Available August, 1983)

楞嚴經淺釋 Zhung Wen. Volume I, $5.00

Sixth Patriarch Sutra - One of the foremost scriptures of Ch'an (Zen) Buddhism, this text describes the life and teachings of the remarkable Patriarch of the T'ang Dynasty, Great Master Hui Neng, who, though unable to read or write, was enlightened to the true nature of all things. ISBN 0-917512-19-7, 235 pgs., $10.00 (Hardcover: $15.00)

Sutra in 42 Sections - *In this Sutra, which was the first to be transported from India and translated into Zhung Wen, the Buddha gives the most essential instructions for cultivating the Dharma, emphasizing the cardinal virtues of renunciation, contentment, and patience.* ISBN 0-917512-15-4, 114 pgs., $4.00

Sutra of the Past Vows of Earth Store Bodhisattva - *This Sutra tells how Earth Store Bodhisattva attained his position as one of the greatest Bodhisattvas, foremost in vows. It also explains the workings of karma, how beings undergo rebirth, and the various kinds of hells. This is the first ·English translation.* Hardcover only, ISBN 0-917512-09-X, 235 pgs., $16.00. *English text without commentary, for recitation, also available.* ISBN 0-88139-502-1, 120 pgs., $6.00.

地藏菩薩本願經淺釋 *Same as the Earth Store Sutra above, including the commentary.* In Zhung Wen,140 pgs., $6.50.

City of 10,000 Buddhas Recitation Handbook 萬佛城日誦儀規 *Has all the material covered in the traditional daily morning, afternoon, and evening services and special services recited in Buddhist monasteries in the East and West. Includes scriptures, praises, chants, mantras, repentances, and so forth.* Bi-lingual edition, Zhung Wen/English 240 pgs., $6.00 (2nd edition).

Vajra Prajna Paramita (Diamond) Sutra - *One of the most popular scriptures, the VAJRA SUTRA explains how the Bodhisattva relies on the perfection of wisdom to teach and transform beings.* ISBN 0-917512-02-2, 192 pgs., $8.00.

COMMENTARIAL LITERATURE:

Buddha Root Farm - *A collection of lectures given during an Amitabha recitation session which explains the practice and philosophy of the Pure Land School. The instructions are very complete, and are especially useful for a beginner.* ISBN 0-917512-08-1, 72 pgs. $4.00.

Great Compassion Dharma Transmission Verses of the Forty-two Hands and Eyes - *Contains 42 b/w photographs of the Venerable Master Hua's self-portrait paintings of the 42 Hands and Eyes, and 42 b/w photographs of copper reliefs of the mudras, with verses by the Venerable Master (with English translation) for each one.* ISBN 0-88139-002-X, 100 pgs., ·$16.00.

Herein Lies the Treasure-trove, *Volume I. Various talks given by the Venerable Master at the City of 10,000 Buddhas during recent years.* ISBN 0-88139-001-1, 250 pgs., $8.50.

Filiality: The Source of Virtue - *Filiality is the very root of Way-virtue. It is the single most vital force that sustains the universe. Therefore, it is only natural that Buddhist disciples base their conduct on an attitude of filial piety and respect, for their parents and elders, for the rulers and officials of countries and the world, for the Triple Jewel, and ultimately, for all living beings, for all beings have at one time or another been our parents.* Vols. I and II of this series contain stories from the 24 famous tales of filial paragons of Zhung Kuo (China), and numerous excerpts from Buddhist Sutras about filial behavior. Vol. I, ISBN 0-88139-019-4, 120 pgs., $7.00; Vol. II, ISBN 0-88139-020-8, 120 pgs., $7.00

Life-pulse of Living Beings - *Instructions on not killing, the detrimental karmic effects and health hazards related to eating meat, and stories of reincarnation concerning these.* ISBN 0-88139-006-2, 250 pgs., $8.50

Listen to Yourself, Think Everything Over - Vols. I and II - *Instructions on how to practice the method of reciting the name of the Buddhas and Bodhisattvas, along with a straightforward explanation of how to cultivate Ch'an meditation. All instructions were given during actual meditation and recitation sessions.* ISBN 0-917512-24-3, 153 pgs., $7.00

Shramanera Vinaya and Rules of Deportment - *The Buddha instructed his disciples to take the Vinaya (the Monastic Moral Code) as their master once he himself had entered Nirvana. This text, by Great Master Lien Ch'ih of the Ming Dynasty, explains the moral code for novice Monks and Nuns.* ISBN 0-917512-04-9, 112 pgs., $4.00

沙彌律儀要略釋　　Same as Shramanera Vinaya, *including the commentary. In Zhung Wen.* 105 pgs., $5.00

Shastra On The Door to Understanding The Hundred Dharmas - *A text fundamental to Consciousness Only doctrine, by Vasubandhu Bodhisattva, with commentary by the Venerable Master Hua.* ISBN 0-88139-003-8, 130 pgs., $6.50

Shurangama Mantra Commentary - 楞嚴咒疏句偈解
Verses and commentary by the Venerable Hua on this Ancient text explaining how to practice the foremost mantra in the Buddha's teaching, including a line-by-line analysis of the mantra. The first volume contains all the instructions on how to prepare before holding the mantra and an explanation of the first portion of the mantra. ISBN 0-917512-69-3, 296 pgs., $8.50 (Bi-lingual, Zhung Wen and English). Vol. II contains an explanation of lines 30-90 of the mantra. ISBN 0-917512-82-0, 200 pgs., $7.50, Vol. III, lines 91-145, ISBN 0-917512-36-7, 160 pgs., $6.50. Vol. IV, Available Summer, 1983.

楞嚴咒疏　　Text of the above, *without the commentary of the Venerable Master Hua. In Zhung Wen,* $5.00

Song of Enlightenment - *The famous lyric poem of the state of the Ch'an Sage, by the Venerable Master Yung Chia of the T'ang Dynasty. (Available Summer, 1983)*

永嘉大師證道歌詮釋 - *same as above in Zhung Wen, with commentary.* 40 pgs., $2.50

The Ten Dharma Realms are not Beyond a Single Thought - *Eloquent poems composed by the Venerable Hua, on all the realms of being, which are accompanied by extensive commentarial material and drawings.* ISBN 0-917512-12-X, 72 pgs., $4.00

Water-Mirror Reflecting Heaven - *An essay on the fundamental principle of cause and effect, with biographical material on contemporary Buddhist cultivation in Zhung Kuo. Clear and to the point; very readable for young and old.* ISBN 0-88139-501-3, 82 pgs., $4.00

水鏡回天錄 - *Same as* Water-Mirror *above, with the commentary. In Zhung Wen.* 130 pgs., $5.00

宣化上人開示錄(一)- *Instructional talks in Zhung Wen.* 190 pgs., $5.00

宣化上人開示錄(二)- *Volume 2,* $6.50

宣化上人偈讚錄 - *Verses in Zhung Wen, including verses for each of the 84 lines of the Great Compassion Mantra.* 150 pgs., $5.

萬佛城聯語集 - *Matched couplets by cultivators at the City of 10,000 Buddhas. In Zhung Wen.,* 82 pgs., $4.00

BIOGRAPHICAL:

Pictorial Biography of the Venerable Master Hsü Yün - *Prose and verses written by the Venerable Hua illustrated with brush drawings, documenting Venerable Yün's life. Will be a two-volume set. Volume 1 contains 104 sections of prose, verses, and drawings. Volume 2 contains 208.* ISBN 0-88139-008-9, 120 pgs., $7.00

Records of High Sanghans - *A living tradition is sustained to the extent that it is embodied in its heroes. The Buddhist tradition is enhanced by a large body of literature containing truly moving and inspiring life-stories of monks and nuns who dedicated their bodies and lives to the preservation and propagation of the Sagely Teachings. Vol. 1 will cover the life-stories of the first eminent Sanghans who brought the Buddhadharma from India to Zhung Kuo, and the adventures of those first Sanghans who withstood severe trials and hardships as they translated the first Sutras from Indian languages into Zhung Wen (Chinese).* ISBN 0-88139-012-7, 158 pgs., $7.00

Records of the Life of the Venerable Master Hsüan Hua - *The life and teachings of the Venerable Master from his birthplace in Zhung Kuo to the present time in America:*

Volume One, *covers the Ven. Master's life in Zhung Kuo.* ISBN 0-917512-07-3, 96 pgs., $5.00 (*Also available in Spanish,* $8.00).
Volume Two, *covers the events of the Master's life as he cultivated and taught in Hong Kong, containing many photos, poems, and stories.* ISBN 0-917512-10-3, 220 pgs., $8.00

Further Volumes Forthcoming

宣化禪師事蹟 - *A separate biographical work in Zhung Wen covering the Venerable Master's life in Zhung Kuo and Hong Kong.* 84 pgs., $4.00

Three Steps, One Bow - *The daily journal of American Bhikshus Heng Ju and Heng Yo, who, in 1973-74, made a pilgrimage for world peace from Gold Mountain Monastery in San Francisco to Seattle, Washington, making a full prostration every third step. The pilgrimage was inspired by monks in ancient Zhung Kuo, who would bow every third step for thousands of miles to a famous monastery or renowned teacher.* ISBN 0-917512-18-9, 160 pgs., $5.00

World Peace Gathering - *A collection of instructional talks on Buddhism commemorating the successful completion of the bowing pilgrimage of Bhikshus Heng Ju and Heng Yo.* ISBN 0-917512-05-7, 128 pgs., $5.00

News From True Cultivators - *The letters written by the two "Three Steps, One Bow" monks (Dharma Master's Sure & Ch'au), during their bowing pilgrimage, addressed to the Venerable Abbot and the Assembly of the City of Ten Thousand Buddhas, are uplifting messages to those traversing the Path of cultivation and inspiring exhortations to all those concerned with evolving vital and workable methods to alleviate the acute problems of our troubled times. The language is simple, the insights are profound. No one should miss reading this book.* ISBN 0-88139-016-X

With One Heart Bowing to the City of 10,000 Buddhas - *The moving journals of American Bhikshus Heng Sure and Heng Ch'au, who made a "three steps, one bow" pilgrimage from Gold Wheel Temple in Los Angeles to the City of 10,000 Buddhas, located 110 miles north of San Francisco, from May, 1977, to October, 1979.*

> Volume One, May 6 - June 30, 1977. ISBN 0-917512-21-9. 180 pgs.,$6
> Volume Two, July 1 -October 30,1977. ISBN 0-917512-23-5, 322 pgs., $7.00
> Volume Three, October 30 - December 20, 1977. ISBN 0-917512-89-8, 154 pgs., $5.00
> Volume Four, December 17 - January 21, 1978. ISBN 0-917512-90-1, 136 pgs., $4.00
> Volume Five, January 28 - February 18, 1978. ISBN 0-917512-91-X, 127 pgs., $4.00
> Volume Six, February 19 - April 2, 1978. ISBN 0-917512-92-8, 200 pgs., $6.00
> Volume Seven, April 3 - May 24, 1978. ISBN 0-917512-99-5, 160 pgs., $5.00
> Volume Eight, May 24 - September, 1978. ISBN 0-917512-53-7. 232 pgs., $7.50
> Volume Nine, September - October, 1978. ISBN 0-88139-016-X, 232 pgs., $7.50

Further Volumes Forthcoming

修行者的消息   -*The complete collection of letters written by Bhikshus Heng Sure and Heng Ch'au during their 2½ year bowing pilgrimage to the City of 10,000 Buddhas; In Zhung Wen. Two-volume set,* $10.00

精進者的日記 (一)   - *Part One of the Journals of the Bowing Monks; in Zhung Wen,* $6.00

精進者的日記 (二)   -*Part Two of the Journals of the Bowing Monks; in Zhung Wen,* $6.50

Open Your Eyes; Take a Look at the World - *The Journals of Bhikshus Heng Sure and Heng Ch'au, and Bhikshuni Heng Tao, written during the 1978 Asia-region visit by the Venerable Master and other members of the Sino-American Buddhist Association.* ISBN 0-917512-32-4, 347 pgs., $7.50.

放眼觀世界   - *Same as* Open Your Eyes...; *in Zhung Wen,*
347 pgs., $7.50.

Heng Ch'au's Journal - *An account of the remarkable experiences and changes undergone by Bhikshu Heng Ch'au when he first came in contact with Gold Mountain Monastery.* 112 pgs., $1.95.

CHILDREN'S BOOKS

Cherishing Life - *Contains verses and brush drawings about not taking life, and public records about cause and effect drawn from actual events recorded by Dharma Masters, giving people's memories of past lives as animals, and their awareness of the reasons for their retributions of being in the animal realm. For elementary-age children, as well as adults.* ISBN 0-88139-004-6, 150 pgs., $7.

Human Roots: Buddhist Stories for Young Readers - *Has a total of 14 stories from the Buddhist Canon and historical records.* ISBN 0-88139-500-S, 95 pgs., $4.00.

MUSIC, NOVELS, AND BROCHURES

Songs for Awakening - *Words and music of over forty modern American Buddhist songs, indexed according to title and first line, with drawings, woodcuts, and photographs. The picturesque, 9" X 12" Songbook makes a fine gift to introduce your friends to Buddhism.* ISBN 0-917512-31-7, 112 pgs., $7.95.

Awakening - *Recorded on cassette tape, ten Buddhist songs set in Western style (all in English), ranging from pop to rock, to folk and country. Subjects covered include: Bodhisattva vows, the I Ching, Ch'an meditation, Lao-Tzu, the Lotus Sutra, an Abhidharma meditation, Amita Buddha and his Pure Land.* $7.00 plus $1.00 shipping in the U.S.A. and $2.00 for international orders.

The Three Cart Patriarch - *A 12" stereo lp., recorded by and for children, based on the "Monkey" tales of Zhung Kuo which features stories, six musical productions, and many special effects.* $7.00 plus $1.00 shipping in the U.S.A. and $2.00 for international orders.

City of 10,000 Buddhas Color Brochure - *Over 30 color photos of the scenic center for world Buddhism, along with many poems and a description of its activities.* 24 pgs., $2.00.

Dharma Realm Buddhist University Catalog, 1983 - ISBN 0-88139-000-3, 246 pages., $5.00. (Available Summer, 1983)

Celebrisi's Journey - *A novel by David Rounds, describing the events in a modern American's quest for enlightenment.* (First edition) ISBN 0-917512-14-6, 178 pgs., $4.00.

荼佛城皇釗善提海

VAJRA BODHI SEA

Vajra Bodhi Sea *is a monthly journal of orthodox Buddhism, which
has been published by the Sino-American Buddhist Association since
1970. Each issue contains the most recent translation work of the
Buddhist Text Translation Society. Each issue includes a biography
of a great Patriarch of Buddhism from the ancient past, sketches of
the lives of contemporary monastics and lay-followers around the
world, a Sanskrit lesson, articles on practice, and other material.
The journal is bi-lingual, in Zhung Wen and English with 24 pages
each, in an 8½" by 11" format. Single issues $2.50; one year sub-
scription $26.00; and three years subscription $70.00. ISBN 0-507-
6986 (postage is included in the subscription fee).*

POSTAGE AND HANDLING

United States - $1.25 for the first book and $.40 for each additional book. All publications are sent via special fourth-class.
Allow from 4 days to 2 weeks for delivery.

International - $1.50 for the first book and $.75 for each additional book. All publications are sent via "book rate" or direct
mail sack (surface). For countries, such as Indonesia and Malaysia,
in which parcels may be lost, we suggest orders be sent via regis-
tered mail for an additional $3.25 per parcel of 10 books each.
We cannot be responsible for parcels lost in the mail. Allow 6 to
8 weeks for delivery.

The rates noted above for postage and handling are given as an indication of actual costs. On large orders, purchasers may wish to
submit their order for a more precise estimate of postage and
handling costs.

All orders require pre-payment before they will be processed.

中文佛書目錄

大方廣佛華嚴經十地品淺釋（平裝三冊） 美國萬佛城宣化上人講解。

第一冊（第一歡喜地） （漢英對照） 定價美金七元。

第二冊（第二離垢地。第三發光地。第四燄慧地。第五難勝地） 定價美金五元。

第三冊（第六現前地。第七遠行地。第八不動地。第九善慧地。第十法雲地）定價美金六元

千手千眼大悲心陀羅尼經（全一冊） 定價美金六元。

般若波羅蜜多心經非台頌解（全一冊） 美國萬佛城宣化上人講解 定價美金五元。

楞嚴咒疏句偈解（漢英對照）（第一冊） 美國萬佛城宣化上人講解 定價美金八元五角。

梵網經講錄（漢英對照）（上冊） 慧僧法師述 定價美金十元。

梵網經講錄（漢英對照）（下冊） 定價美金八元

地藏菩薩本願經淺釋 定價美金六元五角

佛書部分：

永嘉大師證道歌詮釋（全一冊） 美國萬佛城宣化上人講解 定價美金二元五角。

緇門崇行錄 蓮池大師著 弘一大師集 （贈閱）

宣化上人偈讚開釋錄（全一冊） 定價美金五元

宣化禪師事蹟（全一冊） 定價美金四元。

放眼觀世界（亞洲弘法記）、（全一冊） 定價美金七元五角

修行者的消息（三步一拜兩行者一心頂禮萬佛城之來鴻） 定價美金七元

佛教精進者的日記 （平裝上冊） 定價美金六元。

總流通處：

法界佛教總會萬佛城
The DHARMA REALM Buddhist
  Association, INC.
Headquarters: City of Ten
  Thousand Buddhas
P.O.BOX 217, Talmage,
Talmage, CA 95481, USA
Tel: (707) 462-0939

三藩市分會金山禪寺
San Francisco Branch: Gold
  Mountain Monastery
1731 15th Street
San Francisco, CA 94103
Tel: (415) 626-4204, 861-9672

三藩市國際譯經學院
The International Institute for
  the Translation of Buddhist Texts
3636 Washington Street
San Francisco, CA 94118
Tel: (415) 921-9570

洛杉磯分會金輪寺
Los Angeles Branch: Gold Wheel
  Temple
1728 W. 6th Street
Los Angeles, CA 90017
Tel: (213) 483-7497

萬佛城聯語集（一）　定價美金四元
水鏡回天錄（全一冊）美國萬佛城宣化上人著　定價美金五元
沙彌律儀要略解（全一冊）美國萬佛城宣化上人講解　定價美金五元
楞嚴咒疏句偈解（漢英對照）（第二冊）　定價美金七元五角
宣化上人語錄　定價美金五元

即將出版：
大方廣佛華嚴經淺釋（十定品至入法界品）
大佛頂首楞嚴經淺釋
佛教精進者的日記（下冊）

法界佛教總會法界大學出版